HMHS Britanı

GW00503301

The Last Titan Simon Mills

For Lesley

Introduction

When this book was first published in November 1992 I ended the first introduction by saying that I hoped it would serve as a starting point for further investigation into the story of the *Titanic*'s forgotten sister ship. Since then I'm pleased to say that interest in the *Britannic* has been stimulated to such an extent that this book is now enjoying its second edition.

It would be nice to think that this book has played a small part in the *Britannic*'s revival, though I suspect that Dr Robert Ballard's expedition to the wreck in September 1995 also has a great deal to do with it. Yet, although having been fortunate enough to be part of the expedition's historical team, I suddenly find myself wondering if it was such a good idea after all. Before we had even left the Kea Channel there were reports in the *Sunday Express* of a plan by Greek divers to salvage the *Britannic*. True I had wanted to raise the profile of the *Britannic*, but this was most definitely not what I had in mind. I had never for a moment thought that in some way I would be helping to endanger the very ship that I had hoped to preserve. Then again, perhaps I had, but didn't want to admit it to myself.

Be that as it may, hopefully my fears that the *Britannic* may suffer the same fate as the *Titanic* or the *Lusitania* are groundless. The *Britannic* lies well within Greek coastal waters so she can be easily protected, while her status as a war grave and that, even today, the wreck is owned by the British Ministry of Defence should ensure that any attempt to profit from raising either the ship or any artefacts should be doomed to failure.

I hope I can still confidently say that the *Britannic*'s future still looks to be secure. Although it would be foolish to think that the ship will ever enjoy the mystique of the *Titanic* I, for one, think that the story of the *Britannic* is about to enjoy a revival that will make her anything but the forgotten sister.

Simon Mills
June 1996

Contents

ISBN 1 900867 00 1
© Simon Mills, 1992 and 1996
Simon Mills has asserted his right under the Copyright, Designs and Patents Act, 1988, to be identified as Author of this Work.
First edition, 1992, reprinted, 1994
Second edition, 1996
Typeset by PageMerger, Southampton and M-J-P, Doveridge, Derbyshire. Printed By Amadeus Press, Huddersfield, Yorkshire
Published by
Shipping Books Press
P O Box 30, Market Drayton, Shropshire TF9 3ZZ, England
Tel: 01630 652641 Fax: 01630 653181

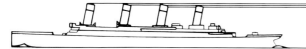

Chapter One

"...Down To The Sea In Ships" (Psalm 107, v23)

The story of the *Britannic* really begins with the death of Thomas Henry Ismay on 23rd November 1899.

Born in 1837, he had become a successful ship owner in his own right before buying the houseflag and goodwill of the bankrupt White Star Line in 1867, continuing the company's proud traditions on the routes from England to Australia. Two years later, with the financial backing of Gustav Schwabe, he registered the Oceanic Steam Naviga-tion Company and at the beginning of 1871, commenced the White Star steamer service on the North Atlantic, where they would eventually become best remembered.

By the end of the nineteenth century, the White Star Line in partnership with the Belfast shipy-ard of Harland and Wolff had secured their reputations going from strength to strength in a peri-od when British industrial power, for so long the envy of the world, was at last coming under serious competition from abroad. One by one the foreign powers began to catch up and overtake British tech-nology in the important heavy industries, but despite the conti-nuing loss of leadership in one staple industry after another, Brit-ish shipbuilding and marine engineering remained unsurpassed and continued to lead the world in innovation and design.

In fact British industrial ca-pacity and maritime tradition had lead to a total transformation in the shipbuilding industry during the second half of the nineteenth cen-tury. The metamorphosis from wooden to iron and eventually steel hulls along with the conti-nued improvments in the design and economy of steam boilers and

Joseph Bruce Ismay became the guiding in-fluence of the White Star Line after the death of his father in 1899.   *Reprint of Shipbuilder*

marine engines meant that by the end of the century the transition from sail to steam power was virtually complete.

The first White Star liner, the *Oceanic* of 1871, had a gross tonnage of 3,707 tons and although steam powered still required the use of sail power to increase her speed and serve as back-up in case of any mechanical failure. Less than thirty years later the second *Oceanic* powered exclu-sively by two triple expansion engines generating some 28,000 HP would become the largest ship in the world at 17,272 gross tons; over four and a half times larger in only twenty eight years.

But by then the competition was beginning to catch up. Between 1892/4 British shipyards had accounted for some eighty per cent of the gross tonnage of merchant vessels launched, but by 1900/04 this figure had fallen to less than sixty per cent of the world share.

To rub salt into the wound, by the end of the century the German ships were also beginning to take the top honours in speed records on the North Atlantic and sud-denly British pre-eminence in their one remaining traditional stronghold was under threat.

It was from this background that the *Olympic*, *Titanic* and *Britannic* ultimately evolved, but the catalyst that finally lead to their conception actually came from the other side of the Atlantic.

In 1901, the great American financier John Pierpont Morgan arrived in the world of shipping. Already a form-idable financial and industrial force on the American continent, he now decided that the time had come to turn his attention to establishing American (or his own?) superiority on the oceans. Taking advantage of a rate war be-tween the leading shipping companies, in a short space of time he had used his own impressive resources to gain control of one shipping line after another and by 1902 the International Mercantile Marine (IMM) had gained control of the American, Atlantic Transport, Dominion, Inman, Leyland, Shaw Savill and Albion and Red Star Lines. With T.H. Ismay now dead, Morgan also successfully completed the acquisi-tion of the White Star Line in December 1902 and the alarm bells in Whitehall finally started ringing.

The growing foreign control of so many British merchant fleets was not only a blow to British ma-ritime pride but could potentially result in a considerable loss of car-rying capacity to the Government in the event of any national emer-gency. The loss of the White Star Line was only off-set after an agreement was signed guar-anteeing that the ships would remain on the British register and at the disposal of the British Government in any emer-gency provided that in turn the British Government would not discriminate against the White Star Line as a foreign controlled shipping line.

If the Government action had been too late to save the White Star Line, at least a number of officials at Whitehall realised that any further attempt by Morgan to gain control of other shipping lines had to be checked. The few shipping lines that were not controlled by the Morgan combine were not long in coming to terms with him and stability returned to the rates on the shipping routes. Only the French Com-pagnie Générale Transatlantique and the British Cunard Line remained completely independent, but with the CGT enjoying financial assistance from the French Government

Above: The first *Britannic* of 5,004 tons entered service in 1874 and served in the White Star fleet for twenty-eight years.

Reprint of Shipbuilder
White Star

Below: The White Star Line offices at James Street in Liverpool.

the position of the Cunard Line was tenuous to say the least.

In an attempt to improve the British position, an appeal for help by Lord Inverclyde, the chairman of Cunard, was viewed sympathetically and Parliament agreed to a loan of £2,600,000 for the construction of two giant superliners that would ultimately become the *Lusitania* and *Mauretania*. The ships had to be capable of maintaining an average speed of at least 24.5 knots and were to be constructed to Admiralty specifications so that they could be taken over as armed merchant cruisers in event of war. Cunard also had to give guarantees that the company would remain under British ownership.

The *Lusitania* was ready for her maiden voyage in September 1907 and was an immediate sensation. At 31,550 tons she was the largest vessel in the world and by regaining the Blue Riband for Britain on her second voyage effectively reasserted British supremacy on the North Atlantic. Two months later she was joined by her sister ship *Mauretania*, slightly larger at 31,938 tons and as time would tell also marginally faster.

With these two new vessels Cunard clearly lead the field on the North Atlantic. Faced with the reality that the Cunard ships were now superior to the White Star ships in every respect, the White Star Line began to plan their response.

One evening, in 1907, Joseph Bruce Ismay, chairman of the White Star Line and president of IMM since 1904, dined at the London home of William Pirrie. Lord Pirrie was the chairman of the Belfast shipbuilders Harland and Wolff, the birth place of the entire White Star fleet and between them they began to draw up their own plans for two super liners and once more regain the initiative.

Although the White Star Line had long since withdrawn from the expensive race to make their ships the

The new Cunard steamer *Lusitania* at speed on her trials in 1907.   *Imperial War Museum*

fastest in the world, instead concentrating on making them the steadiest and most luxurious, the differential in speed could only be allowed to stretch so far. The *Lusitania* and *Mauretania* were capable of over twenty five knots wheras the White Star Line's latest ship, the *Adriatic* of 24,541 tons only had a service speed of a little over sixteen knots; too slow if the company was going to offer a credible express service. The new vessels would clearly have to be considerably faster than the *Adriatic*, but there was still no intention of competing for the Blue Riband.

The two new vessels being larger and faster than any previous White Star ship would present Harland and Wolff with a considerable logistics problem as they did not have a building slip large enough to take one, let alone two vessels of such a huge size. Before construction could begin the shipyard would have to embark on a costly expansion of the facilities at Belfast.

This wasn't the first time that the Belfast shipyard had made alterations to accommodate the construction of White Star vessels. When Thomas Ismay ordered the first four ships for the White Star Liverpool/New York service, the slipways had to be specially constructed and then further strengthened when the *Britannic* and *Germanic* were ordered three years later. Before the *Teutonic* and *Majestic* had been constructed, the shipyard had to be expanded again and two completely new slips built, not to mention the construction of the Alexandra graving dock to accommodate the new generation of liners. Now once more the White Star Line were planning two ships the like of which the world had never seen and once again Harland and Wolff were expanding their facilities to maintain their position as one of the leading shipbuilders in the British Isles, which in effect meant the world.

They were embarking on a scale of construction never before heard of. The *Lusitania* had been constructed at the Clydebank shipyard of John Brown & Co wheras the *Mauretania* had been built on the Tyne by Swan Hunter & Wigham Richardson. But not only were Harland and Wolff going to build both White Star liners, but they would be built at the same time.

To handle the proposed construction, first of all two new building slips had to be built on an area that had

previously been occupied by three. Above the two new slipways a huge gantry 840 feet long and rising to a height of 180 feet was built by the Arrol Engineering Company of Glasgow, complete with cranes and elevators. By the time the slipways were completed each was capable of constructing vessels of up to 990 feet.

But construction of the new slipways was only the first phase and to help with the fitting out of the two ships after launching, a huge floating crane built by the German Benrather Company, capable of lifting 150 tons over 130 feet in height had to be purchased as no other crane in the yard was capable of handling some of the loads that would be necessary.

By the time the work was completed, Pirrie had spent over £130,000 before either of the two keels had been laid. This already huge sum did not include the cost of the new Thompson graving dock being built by the Belfast Harbour Commissioners or the £40,000 already spent by Harland and Wolff on their new ship repair facility at Southampton. Not only was Pirrie spending a fortune on up-grading and expanding the shipyard but the loss in capacity while the work was carried out meant that a number of contracts had to be diverted to other yards. But by the end of 1908 the slipways were complete, the crane had been delivered and at last everything was ready.

To finance the actual construction of the new vessels the White Star Line issued £2,500,000 in new stock to help cover the costs and with the company recording record profits completion was just a formality. On 31st July 1908 the orders for yard numbers 400 and 401, *Olympic* and *Titanic* were confirmed. The keel of the Olympic was laid before the year was out on 16th December 1908 to be followed some three months later by the keel of the *Titanic* on 31st March 1909.

For the next nineteen months, construction continued at a brisk pace, with work on the *Olympic* preceding the *Titanic* by three months in order to take the pressure off of the machine shops. On 20th October 1910 the *Olympic* was successfully launched and while priority was given to her fitting out, construction on the *Titanic* continued at a slower pace. Successfully completing her trials in Belfast Lough, the *Olympic* was ready to be handed over on 31st May 1911, only thirty months after her keel had been laid.

The same day that the *Olympic* was handed over the *Titanic* was launched from slip number three. At long last the White Star Line's ambition to have their own two giant ships in service was on the verge of being realised and as the *Olympic* made her way to Southampton in a blaze of publicity, work on the fitting out of the *Titanic* began immediately.

The arrival of what was now the largest ship in the world at Southampton sparked a great deal of interest and the preparations for the maiden voyage were closely followed in the press.

At 45,324 gross tons, the *Olympic* had exceeded the tonnage of the *Lusitania* by almost half as much again in a period of a little under four years. This was a staggering leap by any standard and with the White Star reputation for service and fittings, she was clearly going to be an exceptional ship.

The *Olympic* joined the *Oceanic* and *Majestic* on the Southampton to New York service replacing the *Teutonic*, another exceptional ship from twenty two years earlier which was in turn placed on the White Star Canadian service out of Liverpool.

Despite the effects of a coal strike, the *Olympic* was ready for her maiden voyage on time and at noon on 14th June 1911 she left Southampton en route for New York via Cherbourg and Queenstown. On board was J. Bruce Ismay who was eager to inspect his new vessel and suggest any possible modifications that might be incorporated into the *Titanic*, still building at Belfast.

This continuing aspiration to build larger and better ships was not only to the advantage of the passengers but was also sound business sense for the White Star Line. Nevertheless, having regained the initiative once more there was no time to rest on their laurels and they still had to work just as hard to maintain the traditions set by their illustrious founder.

In fact the Cunard Line had hardly been idle during the construction of the *Olympic* and *Titanic*. Aware of the potential created by a ship of this class, they had began to explore the possibilities of constructing their own version shortly after the *Olympic* had been launched; less than a week after the launch of the *Titanic* the first keel plates of the *Aquitania* had already been laid.

To add to the competition, Albert Ballin's Hamburg America Line (HAPAG) were also planning their own even larger trio of ships. The *Imperator*, *Vaterland*, and *Bismarck* would all have a projected gross tonnage of over 50,000 tons and with construction of the first vessel already advanced by one year and the keel of the second ship due to be laid in September, there was little time to bathe in the glory that the *Olympic* brought with her.

Considering this situation, discussions had been continuing between Harland and Wolff and the White Star Line for the completion of a third ship of the class to

The main staircase as portrayed in an artist's impression of the time. *Ulster Folk & Transport Museum*

View of the shipbuilders model of the *Britannic*.

Ulster Folk & Transport Museum

compete with the Cunard and German giants. The acclaim that the *Olympic* had received showed that they were clearly thinking on the right lines, but by the time the *Olympic* was ready for delivery no firm order had been made.

Any lingering doubts about the form of the new ship were laid to rest by the *Olympic*'s performance on her maiden voyage. The ship arrived at New York on 21st June, having crossed from Queenstown in 5 days 16 hours and 42 minutes at an average speed of 21.7 knots. Of course this was not nearly fast enough to challenge the speed records set by the Cunard ships but considering that this speed had been attained with five of the boilers not being lit, it was a very impressive performance none the less.

Bruce Ismay was delighted at the reaction to the new ship and wasted no time in cabling Lord Pirrie as soon as the ship reached New York: '*Olympic* is a marvel, and has given unbounded satisfaction.'

Before the *Olympic* had even reached New York, the decision had been made and on 20th June 1911, the order for the third ship of the class was officially completed.

The life of this third ship, although overshadowed by the success and tragedy of her two sister ships, would not be without its own share of controversy, which would actually arise before the vessel had even been launched.

The ship would eventually be named and launched as the *Britannic*, but allegations continue to the present day that the original intended name was *Gigantic*. It does seem likely when placed in context with the names of her two sister ships and even the official history of the Harland and Wolff shipyard supports the allegation.

But following the *Titanic* disaster the choice of a name like *Gigantic* was considered to be embarrassing to the White Star Line and it was subsequently changed to *Britannic*. The alternative name for the new ship was a clever one; not only had the first *Britannic* been a very successful ship for the White Star Line but the name also had a very patriotic ring to it.

Bruce Ismay would later deny that the name *Gigantic* had even been contemplated, but the use of the name in the press before the *Titanic* disaster, even if only speculative, does not really support his denials. It seems to have all the hallmarks of an awkward cover up, though perhaps understandable under the circumstances.

With the order officially confirmed, Harland and Wolff began to assemble the materials that would be needed, but work could not begin immediately because both of the large slipways were already occupied by other contracts.

The launch of the Royal Mail steamer *Arlanza* on 23rd November 1911 finally cleared the space needed for construction to begin and one week later on 30th November the keel of yard number 433, the *Gigantic/Britannic* was laid on the same slipway where the *Olympic* had been built.

If all went according to plan, she would be in service by the summer of 1914.

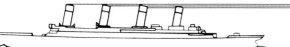

Chapter Two
Back To The Drawing Board

White Star's latest 'Wondership' was also to continue the company's policy of comfort and reliability rather than speed. The public acclaim that the *Olympic* had received showed that this approach was still as successful as the day Thomas Ismay had first made the decision to withdraw from the costly race for higher speed, but with the *Aquitania* threatening to be larger, faster and as luxurious as the *Olympic* not to mention the future threat from HAPAG's even larger trio, the *Britannic*'s interiors would have to be more magnificent than even those of her sisters.

As the third ship of the class, the *Britannic* would incorporate every lesson learnt in the construction and operating of the *Olympic* and *Titanic*. When completed, the resulting hybrid would be a worthy addition to the fleet, in keeping with the White Star tradition of being the first to introduce ever higher standards in accommodation and facilities for passengers of all classes.

Four months after construction began everything was going more or less according to schedule, though only just. On April 2nd 1912, the *Titanic* finally steamed into Belfast Lough to carry out her long delayed trials, departing that same evening for Southampton ready to begin her commercial service.

One of the reasons for the delay in completion of the *Titanic* was the collision between the *Olympic* and the cruiser HMS *Hawke* in the Solent on 20th September 1911. Parts originally intended for the *Titanic* had been transferred to her sister ship in an effort to return her to service as quickly as possible. By the time these parts had been replaced, construction of the *Titanic* had fallen several weeks behind schedule.

The schedule was thrown further out of sync when the *Olympic* again returned to Belfast at the beginning of March 1912 for repairs to a damaged propeller. By the time these repairs had been completed work on the *Titanic* was even

The hull of the *Britannic* fully framed, photographed from the roof of the drawing office of Harland and Wolff in April 1913.
Ulster Folk & Transport Museum

The novel lifeboat arrangements on the *Britannic* were a direct result of the *Titanic* tragedy. This view of the boat stations on the stern of the builders model give the best impression of the size of the new type of davits. *Ulster Folk & Transport Museum*

further behind, leaving the White Star Line barely a week between taking delivery of the new ship and her arriving at Southampton to prepare her for the maiden voyage on April 10th.

While the attention of the press was focussed on the new leviathan at Southampton, construction of her successor quietly continued at Belfast. Less than two weeks later, disaster struck.

At 11.40 pm on April 14th 1912, the *Titanic* collided with an iceberg four and a half days into her maiden voyage from Southampton to New York. Two hours and forty minutes later she foundered taking with her 1502 passengers and crew.

To the shipping lines, not to mention the world, it was a massive shock. The *Titanic* was supposed to represent the latest state of the art in shipbuilding and yet the 'unsinkable' ship costing £1,500,000 had gone down in less than three hours.

For the *Britannic*, this could only mean that major alterations needed to be considered in her designs and while the full implications of the changes were determined, work on the incomplete hull was suspended.

The inquests into the greatest maritime disaster in history were not long in coming. On April 19th, barely twelve hours after the Cunard liner *Carpathia* had arrived at New York with the 705 survivors, Bruce Ismay, who had himself escaped in the last boat on the starboard side, was summoned before a Congressional Committee investigating the disaster, chaired by Senator William Alden Smith of Michigan.

On the other side of the Atlantic the British were a little slower off the mark, appointing Lord Mersey as Wreck Commissioner on 23rd April before the Court of Enquiry commenced on 2nd May.

Against a background of charges of 'farce' and 'whitewash', the American Report was completed less than six weeks after the disaster with the British report following some two months later.

Of the two, Smith was the more wide ranging and certainly more particular in his criticism of individuals and authorities. Captain Smith of the *Titanic* was singled out for 'over confidence', the emergency routine on board was described as 'haphazard' and the British Board of Trade was severely censured for its out of date regulations regarding lifeboat capacity. Lord Mersey on the other hand was much more discreet in his fault finding, concentrating more heavily on the technical aspects of the disaster.

The only individual who came in for universal censure in both reports was Captain Stanley Lord of the Leyland liner *Californian*. Both enquiries decided that unidentified rockets seen from the bridge of the *Californian* on the night of the disaster had been the distress rockets fired from the *Titanic* as she was sinking. Not recognising them as distress signals, Lord had failed to act and as a result over 1500 people had died.

The arguments over Lord's culpability as to whether or not the ship observed from the *Californian* was indeed the *Titanic* and could he have arrived in time even if a rescue attempt had been made continue to the present day. But to the American and British press of 1912, Stanley Lord was the captain who had refused to go to the aid of a ship in distress when he may have been close enough to save the lives of everyone on board.

Recriminations aside, between them the two reports did agree on the necessary measures to ensure greater safety at sea. With the recommended increased water tight sub division and lifeboat capacity for everyone on board worked into the design, construction on the *Britannic* was able to restart.

In the meantime, for the White Star Line, the priority was to ensure that all their ships complied with the new regulations. Immediately after the disaster, Bruce Ismay had ordered that all IMM ships were to be fitted with enough boats for everyone on board. But if public confidence was to be restored in the *Olympic* and *Britannic* then more drastic action was needed.

On 10th October 1912, the *Olympic* returned to Belfast again to have her bulkheads raised and to have an inner skin fitted running the length of the boiler room and engine compartments. In theory the ship would now be able to survive the damage that sank the *Titanic*, being able to float with the first six compartments flooded. Externally, the most noticeable change to her appearance were the extra lifeboats now running the entire length of the boat decks.

In all, the work took over five months and cost £250,000 by the time she returned to service on 2nd April 1913, a year to the day that the *Titanic* had left Belfast on her trials.

Throughout 1913 *Britannic* steadily grew on the stocks but because the *Titanic* disaster had come during such an early stage of construction, the alterations to her final appearance would be far more conspicuous than those of her sister ship.

Although at 852 ft from stem to sternpost the *Britannic* was only marginally longer than the *Olympic*, the addition of the watertight double skin would increase the *Britannic*'s beam by eighteen inches to 94 feet. As on the *Olympic*, the watertight skin ran for the length of the boiler and engine room compartments. Including the fresh water tanks lining the electric engine rooms, this meant that the inner skin,

Above left: This overhead view of the *Britannic* illustrates how far construction had advanced by May 1913, a little over a year after the loss of the *Titanic*.
Above: After the *Titanic* disaster, the lack of a double skin as included in the *Lusitania* and *Mauretania* highlighted a design weakness in the *Olympic* class liners. The inclusion of this extra skin at such an early stage of construction meant that the *Britannic* had some 18" greater beam than her two sisters.
Below: The à la carte restaurant on the *Britannic*. Compare the splendour here with the bare shell of the illustration on page 17. *Ulster Folk & Transport Museum*

WHITE STAR
ROYAL MAIL STEAMER
"BRITANNIC"

Nº433

Superb bow view of the fully framed *Britannic* in April 1913.

Ulster Folk & Transport Museum

Hydraulic riveter at work on the hull in May 1913.

Ulster Folk & Transport Museum

itself divided into compartments and rising four feet above the load line, ran for over 60% of the ships length.

There were also major changes in the arrangement of the bulkheads within the ship. An extra bulkhead was added in the electric engine room dividing the ship into seventeen compartments, as opposed to sixteen on the *Titanic*, but more importantly five of these bulkheads now extended as far up as the Bridge deck, some 40 ft above the waterline.

Although larger than the *Olympic* in tonnage, there was still no intention to increase the *Britannic*'s speed and other than a few minor changes there was little difference in the propelling machinery. There were still 24 double ended and 5 single ended boilers, with a total of 159 furnaces. The boiler rooms were also identical in arrangement though the double ended boilers on the *Britannic* were a foot longer, each weighing 105 tons.

The engine arrangements were also very similar. The *Britannic* had two sets of four-cylinder triple-expansion reciprocating engines each capable of developing 16,000 H.P.. After the steam had passed through the reciprocating engines, it could then either pass straight to the condensers or into a low pressure turbine driving the centre screw when at sea.

The design of the *Britannic*'s turbine was considerably different though. The turbine on the *Britannic* was designed and constructed by Harland and Wolff wheras the turbine on the *Olympic* had been built by John Brown & Co. Essentially they were the same in that they could only operate when the ship was steaming ahead, but the real difference was in the size and power. The turbine on the *Olympic* weighed 420 tons and could develop 16,000 H.P.. The turbine on the *Britannic* was capable of developing 18,000 H.P. and if it was not the most powerful marine turbine afloat, at 490 tons it was certainly the largest.

With a total of 50,000 H.P. the *Britannic* was more than capable of maintaining her service speed of 21 knots with reserve power for extra speed when needed.

Externally, the differences between the *Britannic* and her elder sister were more distinct. As on the *Titanic* the forward end of the promenade deck was enclosed with sliding windows after experience with the *Olympic* in 1911 showed that this area of the deck was too exposed in heavy weather. The *Titanic* had been modified shortly before entering service but these windows were never installed on the *Olympic* because the extra boats installed on the boat deck after the disaster would have obstructed the only remaining uninterrupted views for first class passengers.

The stern of the *Britannic* was also considerably different from those of her two sisters. The aft shelter deck was now enclosed so that the third class passengers would have a covered area of exterior deck space, while the hospital was relocated to the area previously occupied on the *Olympic* by the third class smoke room. The smoke room was then placed above the third class general room adding to the already larger looking stern.

Two other alterations to the deck houses were the

Above: By the summer of 1913 the *Britannic*'s fully framed hull could be clearly seen beneath the Arrol gantry from the County Antrim side of the River Lagan.

Below: 21st October 1913, and by now the hull of the ship is fully plated. The holes for the scuttles are in the process of being cut out.

Both Ulster Folk & Transport Museum

addition of a children's playroom on the port side of the first class promenade deck, opposite the first class gymnasiumn and the dog kennels on the port side of the fourth smokestack, though as on the *Olympic* this stack was actually a ventilator for the reciprocating engine room. But the most striking external difference between the two ships was the new arrangement of lifeboats on the boat deck.

As a result of the *Titanic* disaster, the *Olympic* had a line of rigid and collapsible lifeboats running the entire length of the port and starboard boat decks. In order to restore some of the open deck space that had been lost due to the extra boats, Harland and Wolff planned to install eight sets of huge 'girder' like davits on the new ship.

The *Britannic* was designed to carry 48 open lifeboats. 46 of the lifeboats would be 34 ft long making them the largest ever fitted on a ship, 2 of them also having their own engines and wireless, but 2 extra 26 ft cutters were also included, one either side of the bridge. The boats were positioned in four groups at strategic points along the boat deck, the original design showing five boats on either side of the first smoke stack, twelve either side of the fourth and an additional fourteen boats on the poop deck. This succeeded in restoring much of the space lost on the *Olympic* which at the same time could be used to assemble the passengers in any emergency, who could then be seated in the boats on the deck before being lowered over the side. The falls were controlled by separate motors so that the boats could be lowered on an even keel and a light was fitted to the end of each davit to help with the operation of the gear at night.

After the *Titanic* safety at sea was a prime concern particularly for the White Star Line and their publicity department lost no time in commending the merits of the new type of lifeboat apparatus. The huge size of the davits meant that not only could the boats be lowered a considerable distance from the side of the ship to take in to account any list, but it also enabled them to transfer boats from one side of the ship to the other. Technically this was true but they neglected to mention that the smokestacks obstructed the davits from leaning too far inboard at four of the eight stations.

The appearance of these lifeboat davits did not exactly enhance the fine lines of the ship but later experience would demonstrate that it was an efficient way of lowering the boats.

Another new safety feature though less evident was a pneumatic tube that ran from the wireless room to the bridge, enabling the wireless operator to send any navigational messages directly to the bridge without having to leave his post. Had this been installed on the *Titanic*, the message from the *Mesaba* warning of the icefield received just two hours before the collision may have reached the bridge and history could well have been different – perhaps.

Internally the layout was similar to the Titanic in that the cabins on B deck continued out to the side of the ship, though there was a promenade area forward of the grand staircase. A new feature also on B deck was a hairdressing salon for the ladies next to the gents barbers shop. The à la Carte restaurant was enlarged at the expense of the Café Parisien and a fourth elevator was installed for the first class passengers amidships behind the third funnel casing running down as far as E deck.

But the improvements and modifications were extended to all classes; a gymnasium was installed within the enclosed aft shelter deck for the second class passengers who also gained the lion's share of the extra open deck space above created by this new roof.

An overhead view of the hull in the gantry in October 1913. By now the shelter deck and focsle have been plated.
Ulster Folk & Transport Museum

To complete the *Britannic*'s many added attractions, a larger proportion of rooms had private bathrooms and the internal plumbing was improved so that hot water could be pumped through almost as soon as the tap was turned on, saving time and water.

Construction continued at Belfast but more slowly than anticipated. In May 1912 White Star had announced that the *Britannic* would be in service by the end of 1913, but due to the extent of the alterations in the design, it was announced in May 1913 that she wouldn't be ready for launching until November that year, though even that was to prove optimistic.

In the meantime, White Star continued their New York service with the *Olympic*, *Oceanic* and the ageing *Majestic* maintaining the primary service from Southampton, and the *Celtic*, *Cedric*, *Baltic* and *Adriatic* operating out of Liverpool.

On 26th February 1914 the *Britannic* was finally ready for launching and despite the cold and drizzly weather, Lord Pirrie was at the shipyard as early as 5.00 am superintending the final preparations.

Early the same morning the SS *Patriotic* of the Belfast Steam Ship Company arrived at the York Dock in Belfast having been chartered to bring over the press and other guests of the White Star Line. As the officials and guests arrived at the shipyard large crowds, undeterred by the weather, gathered along the banks of the River Lagan to watch, many arriving several hours before the launch just to guarantee a good view.

But despite the important guest list including delegations from the Admiralty and prominent local officials, not to mention a young telegraph messenger who arrived with

H1954

Lord Pirrie poses with representatives of the Belfast Harbour Commissioners beside the stern of the completed hull on the day before the launch. In the background on slip no. 3, the stern of the *Statendam/Justicia* is clearly visible

Ulster Folk & Transport Museum

By February 1914 the work on the hull is completed and at last the *Britannic* is ready for launching.

Ulster Folk & Transport Museum

a message for Lord Pirrie and was invited to stay and watch, one prominent name was notably absent.

J.P. Morgan, whose financial muscle created IMM had died in Rome at the end of March 1913. There was also another change in the top management when three months later Bruce Ismay retired (some say he was pushed) as chairman of the White Star Line and president of IMM.

Harold Sanderson had succeeded to both positions and was at the shipyard with the other guests to watch the launch which was scheduled to coincide with the high tide.

At 11.10 am the first rocket was fired to signal the workmen in the yard to knock away the last blocks supporting the keel and to warn any vessels on the river to stand clear. With only the hydraulic steel launching triggers holding the ship on the slipway, a second rocket was fired at 11.15 and the triggers released.

Needing no assistance from the hydraulic rams, the grey painted hull moved down the slipway, secured to the land by three anchors and two cable drags, the passage made easier by over twenty tons of tallow, train oil and soft soap. As an added precaution some of the shipyard workers on board were ready to let go the *Britannic*'s anchor in any emergency, but in the event there was no need and 81 seconds later having reached a speed of 9.5 knots the 24,800 ton hull of the *Britannic* was afloat, having been brought to a halt before travelling its entire length in the water. The *Olympic* by comparison had reached a speed of 12.5 knots and took 62 seconds.

Continuing a long standing White Star tradition there was no launching ceremony. The only outward sign of a special occasion was the company flag flying above the gantry with signal flags beneath spelling out the word 'Success'. One shipyard worker later summed it up by saying: 'They just builds 'er and shoves 'er in.'

As the tugs *Herculaneum, Huskisson, Hornby, Alexandra* and *Hercules* towed the hull to the fitting out wharf in the Abercorn Basin, work immediately began to clear the slipway for the construction of the yard's next commission, yard number 469 for the Red Star line. Meanwhile the guests gratefully retired from the elements to the official receptions at the shipyard and a press luncheon at the Grand Central Hotel.

Harold Sanderson was unable to stay due to a rendezvous with the *Baltic* at Queenstown en route to New York so the reception was chaired by Henry Concanon, one of the managers of the White Star Line.

Throughout the afternoon's celebrations, speeches were made praising the ship as representing: '...the highest attainments in naval architecture and marine engineering.' But amongst the toasts of 'Success to the *Britannic*' there was a tactful silence on the subject of the *Titanic* from the press. All the comparisons were with her luckier sister ship, but although not mentioned the disaster couldn't have been very far from their thoughts.

At 9.35 pm the *Patriotic* left Belfast for Liverpool where R.J. Shelley, White Star's head of publicity had arranged a special train to return everyone to London the next morning.

For the time being, the excitement in the shipyard was over and for Harland and Wolff the immediate task was to transform the empty shell of the *Britannic*, now the largest British ship into the most luxurious afloat and at the same time restore the White Star Line's fortunes on the North Atlantic.

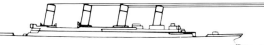

Chapter Three
A Merchant Fleet At War

The launch of the *Britannic* was greeted with the traditional excitement in the newspapers and journals of the day. She was described as: '...a twentieth century ship in every sense of the word...' and: '...the highest achievment of her day in the practice of ship building and marine engineering.'

True the *Britannic* was the fulfilment of the entire experience that Harland and Wolff had acquired since they began building ships in their Belfast yard over fifty years earlier, but the latest lesson had been learnt at a terrible cost.

Two hundred tons heavier than *Olympic* at her launch, the *Britannic* had a projected gross tonnage of 50,000 tons and would have the capacity to carry 790 first class, 836 second class and 953 third class passengers, with a crew of 950.

The fitting out began immediately and as the boilers and heavy machinery were lowered into the hull to be sealed in by the four smokestacks, the ship's waterline slowly began to settle deeper into the water.

At the same time hundreds of engineers, plumbers and electricians worked inside to install the elaborate pipe system, the huge engines and over two hundred miles of electrical cable. As soon as they had finished in one area,

Above: At 11.15 am on 26th February 1914 and 27 months after her keel was laid, the *Britannic* was successfully launched at Belfast.
Below: 81 seconds after the launch, the 24,800 ton hull lies motionless and waiting to be towed to the fitting out wharf.
Both Ulster Folk & Transport Museum

Above: Interior view of the fully plated shelter deck taken in October 1913. The hydraulic riveter on the right is being used to secure the portside deckplates of the bridge deck above, just forward of where the first-class main staircase would be located.

Below: By October 1913 work on the plating of the first-class dining room one deck below on the saloon deck is complete. The deck has been deliberately wetted down to improve the detail on the photograph. *Both Ulster Folk & Transport Museum*

Above: By January 1914 many of the boilers were ready and awaiting collection for lowering into the hull after the ship had been launched.   *Ulster Folk & Transport Museum*

Below: The giant 200 ton floating Benrather crane lowering one of the completed boilers into the empty hull of the *Britannic.* (March 1914).

                                    Ulster Folk & Transport Museum

they were replaced by the carpenters assembling the fine oak panelling and partitions before they in turn made way for the legions of carpet fitters.

But no matter how much time and attention was spent on the *Britannic*'s fittings, for the White Star Line the work still wasn't progressing fast enough.

When the *Britannic* had been launched, it had been reported that she would probably enter service in September that year, remembering that it had only taken seven months to complete the *Olympic* after her launch. In the end this was to prove wishful thinking and on July 2nd 1914 it was announced that the *Britannic* would not be ready for her maiden voyage until the spring of 1915.

Part of the reason for the delay was that Harland and Wolff was now working at full capacity which had not been the case when the *Olympic* had been built. Added to that, problems with supplies and industrial relations were only helping to intensify the problem.

But another more serious reason was that that Harland and Wolff were experiencing pressing financial problems, not made any easier by the small matter of an outstanding £585,000 owed by IMM alone. With rumours abounding of IMM being on the verge of financial collapse, the prospects for the shipyard keeping their biggest customer were not encouraging.

The speculation into the financial security of IMM suddenly seemed to be of little importance when in August 1914, Great Britain, France and Russia declared war on the Central Powers of Germany and Austria-Hungary.

Above: Starboard view of the *Britannic* minus funnels alongside the fitting out basin in March 1914.
Ulster Folk & Transport Museum

Left: The 33 ton Rudder Stock being machined in one of the lathes at Belfast. The completed rudder weighed 102 tons and consisted of five sections held together by some 160 bolts.
Ulster Folk & Transport Museum

The war immediately caused extensive disruption in the shipbuilding industry, with the majority of raw materials being diverted to the shipyards with Admiralty contracts. As Harland and Wolff was not included in this number, work at Belfast continued on the existing civil contracts but at a slower pace.

After three months of hostilites, the shipyard had been forced to lay off over 6000 skilled workers and to compound the problem, many of the men had rushed to enlist before it was too late. Most had assumed that the war would be over by Christmas, but as it became obvious that it was going to last a lot longer than everyone had expected and the need for increased tonnage became more vital to the war effort, the loss of so much skilled labour would later prove difficult to replace.

Despite these problems a certain amount of work could still continue and in early September the *Britannic* was placed in the Thompson graving dock while her propellers were fitted. When the first Admiralty orders finally began to arrive the following month, work on the incomplete merchant hulls had to be placed lower down on the list of priorities.

For the White Star Line the problems were just as great and certainly more immediate. As soon as hostilities had been declared, the military authorities had completely requisitioned the port facilities at Southampton in order to transfer the British Expeditionary Force to France. Not only did the White Star Line have to revert to Liverpool for its American service, but they had to deal with a considerable drop in the number of passengers.

It was just as well that the number of passengers had fallen because Sanderson now suddenly found himself with increasingly fewer ships remaining in his fleet. By the end of 1914, the *Oceanic*, *Celtic*, *Cedric* and *Teutonic* had all been requisitioned as armed merchant cruisers with the 10th Cruiser Squadron, and the *Laurentic* and *Megantic* had been taken for trooping duties. However, with the Admiralty paying for the use of these ships along with other vessels in the combine, the financial problems of IMM were for the time being considerably eased. In the meantime, an improvised service between Liverpool and New York was maintained with the *Baltic*, *Adriatic* and the Red Star liner *Lapland*.

With the *Britannic* safely moored in Belfast, it was also decided to withdraw the *Olympic* from service until the danger had passed and the number of passengers had increased enough to justify the use of such an important vessel. At 11.00 am on October 21st *Olympic* left New York on her last scheduled eastbound crossing before being laid up.

On October 27th, less than a day from her destination at Greenock in the Clyde estuary, the voyage was interrupted off Tory Island on the north coast of Ireland by a distress signal from the British Dreadnought *Audacious* after having struck a mine. Despite the possible risk from enemy submarines and other mines, the *Olympic*'s master Captain Herbert Haddock succeeded in taking the damaged battleship in tow and set a course for the naval base at Lough Swilly.

They nearly succeeded, but as the weather began to worsen the steering gear on the *Audacious* failed causing the tow to part as she sheared off into the wind. At 8.55 pm she blew up and capsized.

Being too dangerous to proceed, *Olympic* was ordered

The reciprocating engines of the *Britannic* erected in the engine shop at Harland and Wolff, before being disassembled for transportation to the hull in the fitting out basin. The smaller engines on the right hand side are destined for the Holland America liner *Statendam/Justicia*.   *Ulster Folk & Transport Museum*

to anchor out of sight of the Grand Fleet in Lough Swilly, and to have no communication with the shore. For security reasons the passengers could not be landed there, but after six days she was cleared to proceed to Belfast, where she arrived on November 3rd.

Captain Haddock's heroic actions had brought him to the attention of Admiral Jellicoe himself, and shortly after the *Olympic* was laid up he was appointed to organise a fleet of merchant ships at Belfast that were to be disguised as warships in an attempt to mislead the enemy.

In the meantime, the *Olympic* and *Britannic* were secured at Belfast where they would remain undisturbed for the next ten months. But although out of sight the two sisters were certainly not out of mind and as 1914 ran into 1915, it became increasingly obvious that sooner or later their services were going to be called upon.

By 1915 the pressures on the merchant fleets due to constant Admiralty demands were stretching the shipping companies to breaking point. Up until then the Admiralty had been reluctant to use the larger ships because of their limitations and cost. The grounding and loss of the *Oceanic* off the Shetland Islands within a month of the outbreak of war had proved how unsuitable ships with a large draught were in coastal waters and the *Aquitania*, originally intended for use as an armed merchant cruiser was laid up soon after being involved in a collision with the Leyland liner *Cana-*

dian with the war being scarcely two weeks old. The *Aquitania* was to remain laid up until she was taken over as a trooper on 18th June 1915.

Part of the reason that the Admiralty could afford to use the larger ships at all was that the Cunard Company had agreed to a special rate of 10/- per gross ton per month for their big ships, as opposed to the original Admiralty estimates of £28,000 per month for the *Aquitania* and £26,000 for the *Mauretania*. This gesture saved the Admiralty over £15,000 per month for these two vessels alone but despite being a remarkably patriotic act, it was also to the benefit of Cunard. By making these concessions, they had retained the use of the larger number of smaller and more useful ships that would have otherwise been taken.

With the *Mauretania* and *Aquitania* both taken for trooping duties to the Dardanelles by June of 1915 and the terrible loss of the *Lusitania* to a German torpedo the previous month, it could only be a matter of time before the two White Star liners would be called up.

For Harold Sanderson, there was no real surprise at this turn of events. In May 1915 he had been informed by Harland and Wolff that the *Britannic* had successfully completed the mooring trials of her engines and could be made seaworthy in something approaching four weeks if the Admiralty were to give her priority. The following month, negotiations with the Admiralty to use the *Olympic* for trooping duties came to nought only because it proved impossible to dry dock the ship before the end of the month due to the tides at Belfast.

But it would only prove to be a temporary reprieve. Sanderson had agreed to the same terms for the *Olympic* that Cunard had negotiated for the *Aquitania*, and on 1st September 1915, the *Olympic* was finally requisitioned for trooping duties. After a hurried fitting out, she was moved to Liverpool and placed in the Gladstone dry dock on September 11th and less than two weeks later on 24th September, His Majesty's Transport *Olympic* (T2810) left Liverpool for her first trooping run to Mudros on the Greek island of Lemnos.

Despite the more widespread use of the larger ships, little progress had been made on the *Britannic* since the outbreak of war. When Harland and Wolff were contracted to convert the merchant ships to dummy warships in October 1914, it became the first of many Admiralty orders culminating in an order for eight Monitors and the 22,000 ton light battlecruiser *Glorious*. The only civil work allowed to continue in the yard had been on the hulls that were nearing the launching stage and even then it was only in order to clear the slipways for new Admiralty contracts.

By the autumn of 1915, the majority of the naval contracts were either finished or nearing completion and

Top right: Detailed view of the steering gear before being installed in the ship.
Right: One of the condensers during assembly. When completed the total combined cooling surface of the two condensers amounted to 50,000 square feet.
Below: The huge 16 ton centre anchor manufactured by N. Hingley & Sons of Netherton, Dudley being hoisted aboard on 3rd April 1914.   *All Ulster Folk & Transport Museum*

Funnel Number 3 leaves the workshop for its journey to the fitting out basin. (April 1914).   *Ulster Folk & Transport Museum*

more attention could be spared on the non military projects until the next Admiralty orders arrived.

If Harland and Wolff were handling their workload with ease, the officials in the Transport Division at the War Office weren't having such an easy time. The horrendous casualties from the Dardanelles campaign had placed an increasing strain on the transport system and in August 1915, the *Aquitania* had been transferred to duties as a hospital ship in the Mediterranean, being joined in the service the following month by the *Mauretania*.

But in the meantime, the casualties continued to mount and it became obvious that even these two giants could not keep pace with the continual stream of wounded. Suddenly the incomplete *Britannic* lying at Belfast began to seem increasingly more attractive and bowing to the inevitable, the War Office accepted that the last giant liner not already in Admiralty service was badly needed. On 13th November 1915, the *Britannic* was finally requisitioned as a hospital ship.

Arrangements were immediately put in hand to prepare the vessel for sea and with the *Britannic* at last having priority, the work continued at a frantic pace. The few luxury fittings that were on board at this time were landed and placed in storage, to be replaced by the more practical fittings necessary in a hospital ship.

The public rooms on the upper decks were ideally positioned for wards so that the wounded would be as close to the boat decks as possible in the event of any emergency, but lower down in the ship the other large public rooms were also put to good use. The central position of the first class dining and reception rooms on D deck made them ideal locations for the operating theatres and main wards. The motion of the ship was least noticeable here and in any emergency, the close proximity of the grand staircase with the three elevators would make access to the higher decks less of an obstacle.

The essential medical personnel would occupy the staterooms on B deck so that they could be as close to the patients as possible, while the cabins on the lower decks were allocated to the remaining medical orderlies and any walking wounded who could then be called upon to form stretcher parties in an emergency.

By the time the work had been completed, there was space on board for 3,309 casualties. Only the *Aquitania* which had space for 4,182 could carry more.

Whilst all this effort was going on to equip the interior of the vessel, there was just as much work to do on the outside. Because of the incomplete condition of the ship, only five of the planned eight sets of davits had been installed. To increase the existing lifeboat capacity six Welin type davits similar to those on the *Olympic* were installed on either side of the boat deck and two more further astern on the poop deck, each handling one open and one collapsible lifeboat. After the war they would be replaced with the girder davits in the original design, but for the time being it meant that there was a total of 58 lifeboats on board.

The paint crews were also working just as hard to transform the exterior. After being laid up for fifteen months the paintwork of the *Britannic* had clearly seen better days and as soon as the corrosion had been cleaned away the hull was freshly painted in the internationally recognized colours of a hospital ship. Before long the entire ship was gleaming from end to end in white paint; to identify her as a hospital ship a green band was painted on each side running from the stem to the sternpost, broken in three places by large red crosses. The funnels were still painted a buff colour similar to the White Star livery but this time there would be no familiar black top.

By day there could be no mistaking the nature of the ship which in theory meant that she would be safe from enemy attack. To ensure her continued safety at night, on each side a line of green electric bulbs ran along the promenade decks with two large red crosses higher up on the boat deck, each lit by 125 electric light bulbs.

The appearance of the ship at night could have quite a profound effect on any observers. On seeing the vessel anchored one evening in the Bay of Naples, Reverend John A. Fleming, the Presbyterian Chaplain on board described

Above left: A sluice valve was fitted in the eduction-pipes between the turbine and the two condensers to enable either condenser to be shut off. *Below:* On 1st August 1914 the 150 ton Turbine Rotor became one of the last pieces of heavy machinery to be hauled aboard. Three days later England declared war on Germany. *Above right:* After delivery alongside in sections, the engines were hoisted aboard to be reassembled in the engine room. (April 1914). *Ulster Folk & Transport Museum*

The engine bedplates en route from the workshops to the fitting out wharf. (April 1914). *Ulster Folk & Transport Museum*

her as: '...a picture from fairyland...' He also went on to say: 'It was not possible, whether by day or night, to mistake the character of the ship.' Or was it?

On the night of 3rd/4th August 1915, the officer of the watch aboard the French steamship *Drôme* observed a red light shining off the starboard bow. Deciding it was the portside navigating light of another vessel, he ordered his ship to be turned to starboard in order to pass the approaching vessel on the port side, which is the correct action when two ships approach each other. But as the *Drôme* began to turn another red light was sighted causing considerable confusion on the bridge of the French ship and soon afterwards the outline of a red cross became visible.

As it turned out, the glare from the electric red cross on the starboard side of an unidentified hospital ship had eclipsed her green starboard navigating light. In mistaking this red light for a port navigating light, the *Drôme* had cut across the bows of the approaching steamer and narrowly avoided being run down.

The French captain was furious that such an incident could occur and wasted no time in sending an official complaint to the Admiralty, who having received similar complaints before decided that the time had now come to actually do something about it.

As a result, an order was issued on December 2nd instructing the port authorities to ensure that the forward red cross on the starboard side of all hospital ships was positioned as far aft as practicable so that it could not interfere with the navigation lights. As an additional safeguard, a switch was to be placed on the bridge so that the captain would be able to turn off the forward starboard cross whenever the ship was in fog or heavy weather. No alteration was considered necessary to the string of green

lights that ran along the sides of the ships because they did not burn brightly enough to obscure the red port side navigating light.

Needless to say, these modifications added to the cost of fitting out a hospital ship came to quite a tidy sum. It had cost £68,000 to fully equip the *Mauretania* and £63,000 to convert the *Aquitania* to a troop ship and then a hospital ship. Another £90,000 was spent on equipping the *Britannic* making a grand total of £221,000 for these three ships alone. This huge sum amounted to more than the entire cost of the first *Britannic* built some forty years earlier, but it was still considerably cheaper-and-quicker-to fit out three large ships rather than a larger number of smaller vessels.

Despite this heavy expenditure, in the long term the Admiralty would still be getting a good deal. The *Britannic* was also chartered to the Admiralty at the rate of 10/- per gross ton per month but at 48,158 tons and thus being some 4% larger than the *Olympic*, the final total would still amount to over £24,000 per month.

The White Star Line also benefitted from the new arrangements with the Admiralty. By this time the Admiralty were also assuming the full cost of insuring the vessels and as an added bonus there could be no arguments about the depreciated value of the ship.

When the *Olympic* had been requisitioned, the Admiralty insisted that for insurance purposes the depreciated value of her first cost should be calculated at 5% per year to ensure parity with the Cunard vessels. Sanderson on the other hand wanted the depreciation calculated at 4% and the problem was only solved when White Star insured the difference in the two totals of £76,279 on the insurance market themselves.

In the case of the *Britannic* there could be no question of her depreciated value as she was of course brand new. After several revisions, the final cost was worked out in March 1917 at exactly £1,947,797.5.10.

But despite this little bonus, Sanderson still could not have the captain that he wanted. When the *Olympic* had been requisitioned he had written to the Director of Transports at the Admiralty to enquire if Captain Haddock could be released from his duties at Belfast to take up the position on his old command. Deciding that Haddock was more valuable where he was, the Admiralty had refused the request and so Bertram Hayes was appointed in his place.

Seven weeks later Sanderson now decided to try and get Haddock appointed to command the *Britannic* and again wrote to the Admiralty, describing him as: '...the very best man in our employ.' Once again the request was denied so Sanderson had to return to his list of suitable commanders.

He quickly decided that the best man for the job was Captain Charles Bartlett, who had been with the White Star line since 1894. Bartlett had received his first command in 1903 and by 1907 he had risen to command the *Cedric*. Since 1912 he had been White Star's Marine Superintendent at Belfast and had been able to monitor the construction of the *Britannic* as she was being built. At the outbreak of war, he had been transferred to patrolling duties in the North Sea so it was unlikely that there would be any problem in getting the Admiralty's consent.

While Sanderson arranged the commander, Harland and Wolff continued the fitting out and true to their word, less than four weeks later *Britannic* was ready for her trials.

On December 6th the Admiralty officially informed the German authorities via neutral American diplomatic channels of the *Britannic*'s status as a hospital ship. Two days later she steamed into Belfast Lough to successfully complete her trials as both the *Olympic* and *Titanic* had done before her, returning to Belfast the same evening to be officially handed over to the White Star Line.

The same day, Henry Concannon officially registered His Majesty's Hospital Ship *Britannic* in Liverpool, the home port of the entire White Star fleet.

On the evening of 11th December, with Harland and Wolff having completed as much of the conversion as possible, the *Britannic* finally left Belfast under the command of Captain Joseph Ranson, arriving at Liverpool the next morning, where she was immediately commissioned as a hospital ship.

Although seaworthy, a great deal of work still had to be completed on the ship as most of the medical supplies and much of the surgical equipment had yet to be installed. By the time all the equipment had been placed on board, the ships surgeon, Doctor J.C.H. Beaumont described her as: '...the most wonderful hospital ship that ever sailed the seas', adding: 'Probably no hospital even on shore had more advantages.'

On 14th December, Captain Bartlett officially assumed command of the *Britannic* and set about the task of preparing the new vessel for her maiden voyage.

One week later the *Olympic* also arrived back in the Mersey having just completed her second trooping run to Mudros.

Two days later, the *Britannic* would be leaving on her maiden voyage to bring many of them back.

The first of the sisters, *Olympic*, at sea, possibly in the Solent.

Imperial War Museum

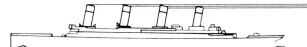

Chapter Four

"...the Most Wonderful Hospital Ship That Ever Sailed The Seas"

The Greek island of Lemnos was the centre of operations for the hospital ships in the Mediterranean. Although it had originally been established as an advance base for the attack on the Dardanelles, the location and port facilities of the island also made it the ideal choice to receive invalids from other less well-known theatres of war.

By the end of 1915, the Mediterranean was criss-crossed with an elaborate network of routes for military transports and hospital ships stretching from Gibraltar, Spezia and Naples in the west to the eastern ports of, Egypt, Salonika, Palestine and of course the beaches of Gallipoli. These routes all converged on the nerve centre of the operation at Mudros and if that wasn't enough, casualties would also arrive regularly from East Africa and India via the Suez Canal. After arriving the invalids were transferred to the already hard pushed military hospitals at Mudros until they could be repatriated in one of the larger hospital ships sent out from England.

The capacity and high speed of the *Britannic* made her an ideal vessel for this service. Such a huge ship could certainly help to contain the medical crisis developing in the Mediterranean, but although the War Office had allocated her to this theatre of operations, she could actually be dispatched any where and at any time as the military situation dictated.

The military activity in France was often unpredictable and in October 1915, the Inspector General of the B.E.F. had written to the Admiralty advising: '...it is absolutely necessary that we should be prepared at short notice to meet an evacuation estimated at between 5,000 and 6,000 cases per day.'

These were frightening figures by any standard but with commitments stretching across the entire globe, the Royal Navy would be hard pushed to meet this obligation, even if it was the largest in the world.

To keep a number of hospital ships idle in the Channel ports on permanent stand by, let alone vessels the size of the *Aquitania* or *Britannic*, just couldn't be justified either economically or militarily. However, by the end of 1915 there were some 64 hospital ships in service and it was accepted that in all probability there would always be some in home ports available for emergency use, though it could never be guaranteed.

This situation meant that as soon as the *Britannic* arrived back from one voyage, the turn around had to be completed as quickly as possible. Even if there was no urgent demand for her return to Mudros the ship always had to be ready to depart for France at short notice.

With the preparations finally completed, the *Britannic* quietly slipped her moorings shortly after midnight on 23rd December and headed out into the Irish sea en route for Mudros. In stark contrast to the colourful maiden voyages of her two sister ships, on the *Britannic* there was no celebration, gaiety or relaxation, but instead a quietly efficient medical staff that had more serious things on their minds than ship's orchestras, dancing or Turkish baths. Although there were no patients to care for on the outward leg of the journey that didn't mean that there was no work to be done. The routine on a hospital ship was laid down in an Admir-

View of hospital ships at Southampton. *Aquitania* occupies a berth in the Ocean Dock in the background not yet in the colours of a hospital ship indicating that this picture was probably taken during the first year of the war.   *Imperial War Museum*

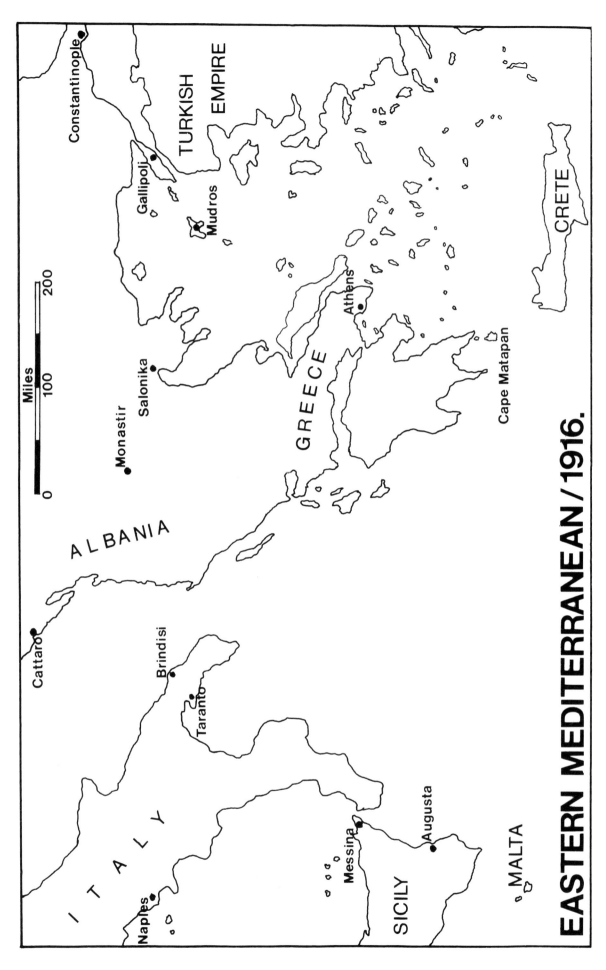

EASTERN MEDITERRANEAN / 1916.

28

One of the military hospitals at Mudros. The bay in the background is filled with military and transport vessels.

Imperial War Museum

alty booklet and the captain and chief medical officer had to run the ship as close to the guidelines as was possible.

Once aboard, the patients and medical staff were subjected to the same daily routine. The patients were woken at 6.00 am and the wards and passageways were immediately cleaned. The patients breakfast was served between 7.30 and 8.00 am after which the tables, benches and W.C.'s had to be cleaned and ready before the captain and senior medical officer made their rounds at 11.00. Lunch normally began at 12.30 after which the wards would again be swept out and the hospital areas disinfected. At 4.30 tea was served and the patients would be put to bed at 8.30 pm before a ship's officer and a medical officer made the final rounds half an hour later.

If this formula resulted in a well coordinated and methodical system, John Beaumont had no doubt what he thought of the regulations, referring to the 'red tape fiend' and adding: 'It seemed to me that the best interests of the patient were nothing in comparison to strict adherence to Regulation no:-, Sub Section:-!'

For the next few days though the routine would not be quite so meticulous as there would be no patients on board until the ship arrived at Mudros. That didn't mean that there was no work to be done and aside from keeping the ship spotlessly clean, everything had to be completely ready to receive the 3,300 casualties by the time the ship reached Naples, which meant that the nurses had a lot of beds to make up.

The *Britannic* duly arrived at Naples, her only port of call before Mudros on 28th December, where she was scheduled to take on enough coal and water to enable her to complete the journey to Mudros and back to England. As a hospital ship, it was important that she completed the journey home when loaded as quickly as possible so she refueled on the outward leg of the voyage.

As a trooper, *Olympic* on the other hand was fully loaded on the way out so she travelled non stop to Mudros. In order that the facilities at Naples were not strained she refueled on the homeward leg of her journey at the northern Italian port of Spezia before returning to England. In an emergency, there were coaling facilities at Mudros but they were almost exclusively reserved for the military.

This procedure not only helped to keep the troops and patients on board for as short a time as possible but over a prolonged period of time could save a considerable sum of money. The Admiralty estimated that for every day the *Olympic* remained anchored with a full complement of troops on board, she would burn an extra 25 tons of coal on top of the 125 tons that would normally be consumed.

With the refueling completed, *Britannic* left Naples at 3.50 pm the next day on the last stage of her journey. After arriving at Mudros on New Years Eve, the transfer of the casualties began at once, continuing over the next four days.

As they were brought aboard, the invalids were detailed to which ever ward was the best suited to their illness or injury by the senior medical officer, Colonel Henry Anderson. Meanwhile the N.C.O.'s from stores issued the walking wounded with hospital suits (blue trousers and jackets with brown facings), at the same time placing their uniforms in the invalids effects room until the ship returned to England. Without these suits the patients were not permitted on deck. The sight of a large number military uniforms on a hospital ship might have led to the

The *Britannic* as a completed hospital ship, number G618.

Ulster Folk & Transport Museum

understandable conclusion by the enemy that she was being used to transport troops.

Fortunately the task was made easier by the fact that the wounded arrived on board having already received emergency treatment, though there were always a constant number of more serious cases needing closer attention. But even the facilities of the finest hospital ship in the fleet couldn't always help and the *Britannic* suffered her first fatality on 2nd January when Private Arthur Howe died of tubercular disease.

For the luckier patients, once aboard they received the best possible care. The large number of casualties each with different illnesses meant that their diets had to be varied, so at 6.00 pm every evening Colonel Anderson would present the purser, Claude Lancaster with the list of provisions needed for the next day. It would be the duty of the ship's chief chef to personally supervise the preparation of these special meals and as a small bonus, any wounded officers were also entitled to a ration of wine or spirits as long as their medical cards permitted it.

When the ship arrived back in England, the accounts were then sent to the Admiralty to be settled with no questions asked.

In contrast the catering on a troop ship was not quite as painstaking, though the White Star Line did try to improve the food rations as much as possible. On the *Olympic*'s first trooping voyage, the expense of feeding the troops came to £9,667.17. 7, but by the time the Admiralty had paid the White Star Line at the negotiated victualling rates, the catering costs actually added up to a loss £2,713.17.10. When Sanderson wrote to the Director of Transports at the beginning of 1916 to suggest a review of the rates, the Admiralty declined to treat the *Olympic* as a special case because it would have been unfair to the other shipping companies.

By 3rd January no more wounded could be taken on board and after the body of Private Howe had been landed for burial, the *Britannic* departed at 3.35 pm on the last leg of her journey, non stop for Southampton.

Aside from the speedy repatriation of the patients, Captain Bartlett had one other official duty to carry out on the journey home by signalling as the ship passed Gibraltar the breakdown of patients into categories of Naval and Military 'cot cases' and walking wounded (Officers and men). It was also necessary to signal the number of dysentry and enteric cases on board, so that the waiting hospital trains at Southampton could be prepared and their destinations worked out in advance.

Due to the regulations concerning hospital ships, this was one of the few occasions on which the ship's wireless could be used. Any signals recieved from a hospital ship were liable to be misunderstood by the enemy which might have endangered the ship; as an added precaution transmissions to hospital ships were also kept to a minimum.

As the ship raced through the Mediterranean another loss had to be recorded in the logbook as the *Britannic* suffered her second casualty. At 6.39 am on 5th January a report came to the bridge that a man had either jumped or fallen overboard. Wartime regulations meant that it was impossible to go back and search for the unfortunate individual and only after the ship itself had been searched was it discovered that a naval rating named Samuel Jones was missing.

At 3.00 that afternoon a court of enquiry was held but whether he had jumped or fallen couldn't be determined with any certainty. Being so far from land his prospects of survival were negligible and the log concluded: '...it is reasonable to assume that he is dead.'

Sadly it was not to be the last death during the voyage when on 9th January, Private Charles Vincent, aged only 21 died of tubercolosis, with the English shore in sight.

Later that day the *Britannic* arrived back at Southampton and immediately began to off-load the wounded. Normally the first to be landed, once their side arms had been returned to them from the strong room, were the wounded officers who were then placed on one of the hospital trains going to London. Then it was the turn of regular troops or ratings who were destined for one of the five provincial medical centres. Whenever possible they were sent to hospitals that were closer to their homes but the priority was to deliver them to hospitals that specialised in treating their specific illness.

Above: Britannic at Mudros. In the foreground is the British battleship HMS *Lord Nelson* and the Admiralty yacht HMS *Triad.*   *Imperial War Museum*

Right: An unusual stern view of the *Britannic* as she arrives at Southampton. The square structure on the stern with the darkened windows served as the ship's mortuary.

Imperial War Museum

The next day the body of Private Vincent was landed while preparations continued for the next voyage.

Shortly before noon on 20th January, the *Britannic* was once more outward bound for the Mediterranean arriving at the navy landing stage of Naples at 7.00 am on 25th January. That evening, having taken on 2,510 tons of coal and 1,500 tons of water, Bartlett signalled to Mudros that he would be ready to depart at 6.00 am the next morning and expected to arrive some time around dawn on 28th January.

But before the ship could depart an order arrived from Cairo instructing that the *Britannic* was to remain where she was and take on wounded from the hospital ship *Grantully Castle*, which had been redirected to Naples while en route for Mudros. The order to proceed to Mudros never came and over the next nine days five hospital ships arrived at Naples to transfer their wounded passengers.

On 28th January 438 invalids were transferred aboard from the *Grantully Castle*, with a further 393 from the hospital ship *Formosa* the same evening. These two vessels departed from Naples on 30th January but were soon replaced by the *Essequibo* on 1st February with 594 wounded on board and the *Nevasa* the next day with another 493 casualties.

In the mean time, the stay at Naples provided the British Consul with an opportunity to prove that the *Britannic* was exactly what she claimed to be.

On 25th January the Duke of Aosta, just back from the Italian front had asked for permission to visit the wounded but at that time there had been none on board. Although the Duke was to be disappointed, it was clear to the British Consulate that the situation could be used to their advantage.

The next day, the American ship *Desmiones* arrived in port. Not wanting to miss a golden opportunity of demonstrating that the *Britannic* was a legitimate hospital ship, Bartlett and Anderson were instructed by the British Consul to invite her captain on board. At the same time the medical staff of the American ship were also invited to inspect the facilities on board and help in the transfer of the wounded when they arrived.

Two days later the American Ambassador Nelson Page, who happened to be in Naples on holiday with his wife and daughter, was also invited to inspect the ship which he duly did, bringing his family on board with him.

While the *Britannic* was in Naples, one enterprising merchant even sent the British Consulate a tender for his company to carry out all over side painting on the ship for £80, which was considerably less than the same work would have cost in a home port, although the White Star Line would have to supply the paint. The estimate was forwarded to the White Star Line via Captain Bartlett but later developments meant that it would never be accepted.

On 30th January orders arrived to return to Southampton as soon as wounded had been taken on from the hospital ships *Essequibo*, *Nevasa* and *Panama*.

The *Panama* finally arrived on the morning of 4th February and the transfer of her 319 casualties was soon underway. Shortly before noon the operation was completed and with no further business, the *Britannic* left Naples at 3.15 pm that afternoon. She arrived at Southampton five days later with all 2,237 wounded safely on board, where she would remain for the next five weeks.

But although temporarily unemployed, the activities on the *Britannic* had become the topic of a diplomatic dispute between London and Rome.

On 1st February a representative of the Neapolitan Sanitary Authorities had boarded the ship in order to inspect the procedures and precautions. Obviously not happy with what he had seen, the Italians had complained to the Admiralty of the use of Naples as a base for transferring patients due to the 'dangers of infection' at the port and suggested that the Sicilian port of Augusta would be more appropriate.

Quite what the inhabitants of Augusta had done to deserve being exposed to these dangerous infections wasn't clear, but perhaps the real reasons for the Italian objections lay elsewhere. Although Italy was at war with Austria she was still officially at peace with Germany and indeed had been a member of the Triple Alliance with Germany and Austria less than a year earlier. The open use of such an important port as Naples for the transfer of Allied wounded may have lead to some protest or reaction from Germany that the Italians would rather have avoided. By offering the Allies the use of the less prominent port of Augusta instead the Italians could for the time being assist their new allies without antagonising one of their old ones.

However, with the Dardanelles by now abandoned, the dangerous journey to Mudros was for the time being no longer so necessary anyway and with few alternatives, the Admiralty decided to explore the possibilities that Augusta offered.

Unfortunately the British naval authorities at Malta did not agree with the Admiralty's decision to use Augusta as a base. Not only were they concerned at the lack of coaling facilities at Augusta but the small number of jetties would make the transfer of casualties from ship to ship more difficult.

But it was also suggested that the opinions of the commanders of the large hospital ships that would have to use the port would be useful. Bartlett advised that the *Britannic* being rather larger than most ships would need to anchor in about 10 fathoms, making her anchorage at Augusta somewhat exposed. The port itself was open to the south east and any strong winds from this direction were likely to hinder the transfer of patients from ship to ship. The exposed anchorage also meant that it would be advisable to have steam up and ready for immediate use while the ship lay there. It was hardly ideal but the problems were by no means insurmountable.

Nevertheless, the Admiralty decided to try anyway and when the *Britannic* departed on her third voyage on 20th March, Augusta was the new destination.

For the third voyage there was not only a new destination, but a new ship's surgeon. John Beaumont had to leave the ship the day before sailing because on the last voyage he had been sick with Paratyphoid B fever and although he had practically recovered, he was still a possible 'carrier' of the disease. It was hardly a fortunate way to escape from the 'red tape fiend' and in his place went Doctor D.W.Stevens Muir, who had been on the *Arabic* when torpedoed seven months earlier.

Arriving at Naples on the 25th March, the *Britannic* took on coal and water as usual. Two days later she departed from Naples and arrived safely at Augusta on 28th March.

Having completed loading, the ship was homeward bound three days later reaching Southampton on 4th April though one of the patients on board, Private Robert Pask of the VIII South Wales Borderers died from Diabetes shortly before the ship arrived. His body was landed for burial after the wounded had been dispatched.

But by now the need for so many hospital ships had passed. With the beaches of Gallipoli now deserted, the constant stream of casualties was for the time being at least considerably reduced and one by one the larger ships were laid up.

The first to go was the *Mauretania*, being paid off on 1st March with Cunard being paid £60,000 to cover the cost of reconditioning her as a liner. The *Aquitania* followed on 10th April with Cunard being paid another £90,000 and two days later the *Britannic* was laid up at Southampton at half rate (5/- per gross ton) until her services were needed again.

With the majority of the crew paid off, the ship remained in the Solent for the next five weeks before financial pressure from the War Office forced the Transport Division to accept that they could no longer afford to keep the ship in service.

Arriving back at Belfast on 18th May, three days later the crew were paid off and assigned to other vessels. Captain Bartlett was allowed to return to his civilian duties with the White Star Line, who were also paid £76,000 to cover the cost of reinstating the liner for commercial service.

Olympic as a military transport at Mudros with the hospital ship *Aquitania* taking on wounded from a smaller hospital ship in the background.

Imperial War Museum

Two weeks later on 6th June the *Britannic* was officially released from Government service.

For the time being, the *Britannic*'s war was over, but shortly before arriving back at Southampton, events that would have a dramatic effect on her future were already beginning to unfold.

On 1st April, the German long range mine laying submarine *U73* under the command of Kapitanleutnant Gustav Siess left Cuxhaven bound for the Mediterranean via the north of Scotland. Passing through the Straits of Gibraltar undetected, Siess had deposited his mines off the coast of Malta, sinking the British battleship *Russell* on 27th April with the loss of 126 of her crew, before arriving at the port of Cattaro (now Kotor) on the Austrian Adriatic three days later.

The following month under American pressure due to the threats to American nationals and neutral shipping, Germany had agreed to revert to Prize Rules in the war at sea and suspended submarines from attacking without warning. This decision may have been influenced by the fact that it gave the German Navy an opportunity to concentrate their submarine forces in the North Sea shortly before the Battle of Jutland.

But if Germany was playing it safe on the North Atlantic, the situation in the Mediterranean with fewer neutral ships to menace remained unchanged and the campaign was if anything intensified.

Although the *Britannic* had safely completed three voyages to the Mediterranean and was for the time being laid up and away from the dangers of war, the future safety of any ships in this theatre of war was becoming bleaker by the minute.

Dr J.C.H. Beaumont, senior surgeon on board *Britannic*.

T.H.S. Archives

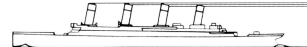

Chapter Five

"The Fog of War"

While the *Britannic* lay at Belfast throughout the summer of 1916 the war continued at an unabated pace. For the time being the military situation in the Mediterranean was under control, but events in France would soon show that the Transport Division's arguments to keep the *Britannic* laid up at half rate rather than pay her off as the War Office instructed were correct.

By the end of the first day of the British offensive on the Somme on 1st July, 1916, the British Army had suffered 60,000 casualties of which 20,000 had been killed. By the time the offensive finally ground to a halt in the middle of November, the Allied armies had gained a little over five miles for the cost of some 600,000 casualties of which over two thirds were British.

Indeed the flow of casualties almost overwhelmed the Channel hospital ships and in the week ending 9th July 1916, 151 hospital trains left Southampton carrying over 30,000 casualties while the reconditioning of the *Aquitania* and *Britannic* for service on the North Atlantic went on undisturbed.

The course of the war at sea was also about to change radically when the British Grand Fleet under Admiral Jellicoe and the German High Seas Fleet of Admiral Scheer finally confronted each other at Jutland on 31st May. Despite being able to inflict heavier losses on the British Fleet, the Germans were so badly mauled that they were forced to discontinue the action and run for home. It would be almost three months before the German fleet was ready to put to sea again and then when reports arrived of the approaching British Fleet they raced for their home ports.

The German failure at Jutland to isolate and destroy a squadron of the British Fleet was to have very far reaching consequences. Realizing that the surface fleet could not win the war at sea for Germany, the decision was made to suspend the construction of capital ships and instead concentrate on building up the submarine fleet. Although not officially declared until the end of January 1917, it was the beginning of the unrestricted submarine warfare for which the German Generals had argued for so long, and would ultimately bring Germany to within an ace of forcing Britain out of the war.

Although the *Britannic* was secure from the threat at Belfast, the war in the Mediterranean was also about to intensify and inevitably the casualties once again began to mount.

Gallipoli was by now abandoned but since October 1915 there had been an Allied army at Salonika in neutral Greece to block German supplies to Turkey and force Germany to divert forces from the Russian front. In the end the Allies actually ended up committing more troops than the enemy and from a small sideshow the Allied forces gradually mounted. By the end of the war almost 500,000 troops had been landed and the Germans were able with some justification to call Salonika 'their largest internment camp'.

The opening of a new Allied offensive at Salonika in September 1916 combined with two other British offensives against the Turkish army in Palestine and Mesopotamia, meant that the hospital facilities at Mudros were once again being placed under extreme pressure and the need for more hospital ships in the Mediterranean became a matter of urgency.

The *Britannic* was the logical choice to be called up first as she had been the last hospital ship to be laid up, consequently her fittings would be more intact. However, the Transport Division in their infinite wisdom decided to call up the *Aquitania* first in spite of the fact that her re-conversion as an ocean liner was largely complete. No doubt the War Office now realised their mistake in not keeping the *Britannic* laid up at half rate in the first place but as the *Aquitania* had a larger capacity and was already at Southampton occupying harbour facilities badly needed by the military authorities it was decided to call on her services first.

On 21st July the *Aquitania* was once again requisitioned as a hospital ship and the Harland and Wolff ship repair facility at Southampton were given the task of undoing all their work to convert the ship for commercial service and refit the vessel as a hospital ship once again.

In the end it didn't really matter which ship was called up first because it soon became obvious that once again the flow of casualties from Mudros was too great for the available hospital ships. On 28th August the White Star Line were once again informed that the *Britannic* was being taken over as a hospital ship.

On 4th September, Charles Bartlett was officially re-appointed as captain and the *Britannic* left Belfast once more to complete the fitting out at Southampton. On 9th September she was moved to an anchorage off Cowes to await orders while a new crew was mustered.

The ship remained anchored in the Solent for over two weeks but finally the order to return to the Mediterranean was issued and at 5.40 pm on 24th September the *Britannic* was once again bound for Naples. She arrived five days later and after taking on coal and water as usual, left the Italian port on 1st October in time to arrive at Mudros on the 3rd.

After two days the transfer of wounded was completed and with no further reason to stay, the *Britannic* left Mudros on 5th October. During the voyage home though one more casualty had to be entered in the log when three and a half hours after leaving Mudros, Corporal Joseph Seddon died of nephicitis and uraemia. This was the only casualty of the voyage and the body was buried at sea at 10.30 the same evening. The remainder of the voyage passed uneventfully and the ship arrived back at Southampton on the 11th.

The next departure was scheduled for only nine days later but as the usual preparations continued at Southampton to get the ship ready for sea, events in London were taking place that would result in the voyage being far from routine.

On 13th October the Transport Division asked the Admiralty if a request by the R.A.M.C. to transport medical personnel and stores in the *Britannic* could be approved. Due to the shortage of time available before the ship was due to leave, the Admiralty agreed to the request three days later but added that in future the only medical personnel that would be transported to foreign stations in a hospital ship would be nurses. The orders were confirmed on 17th October and the R.A.M.C. were instructed to have their stores alongside the ship and ready for loading the following day.

The *Britannic* departed as scheduled at 4.30 pm on 20th October but along with her usual complement of medical staff she had on board medical supplies and personnel for other various theatres of war:

For Egypt:
15 Officers. (R.A.M.C.)
16 Chaplains.
2 Other Ranks. (R.A.M.C.)
1,856 Packages of Medical Stores.
For Malta:
5 Officers. (R.A.M.C.)
1 Chaplain.
10 Female Doctors.
1 Nurse.
2 British Red Cross Members.
1 Other Ranks. (R.A.M.C.)
96 Packages of Medical Stores.
For Salonika:
10 Officers. (R.A.M.C.)
181 Other Ranks. (R.A.M.C.)
168 Tons of Stores.
156 Nurses.
2 British Red Cross Members.
795 Packages of Medical Stores.

For India:
17 Officers. (R.A.M.C.)
52 Nurses.
4 Assistant Surgeons.
8 Dental Mechanics.
1 Other Ranks. (R.A.M.C.)
For Mesopotamia:
15 Packages of Medical Stores.

In all this came to a total of 483 extra medical personnel on board who could not officially claim to be part of the crew along with a large amount of medical and other stores for foreign stations. True these extra personnel were non combattants but whether or not it was permissible for a hospital ship to transport them at all was something of a moot point. It was an issue that the Germans would later use in a list of so called abuses of hospital ships that would ultimately be used to help justify their policy of unrestricted submarine warfare.

The *Britannic* duly arrived at Naples on 25th October and departed at 4.42 pm the following afternoon having taken on 3,000 tons of coal and 2,000 tons of water. After an uneventful voyage she arrived at Mudros at 8.00 am on the 28th and immediately began to off-load her passengers, their places soon taken by the wounded that were awaiting transfer back to England.

Over the next two days 3,022 casualties were taken aboard from six hospital ships including the *Dunluce Castle*, *Glenart Castle*, *Llandovery Castle*, *Grantully Castle* and *Valdivia*.

Also included in this number was the hospital ship *Wandilla* which had arrived from Malta with invalids destined for England. But amongst the invalids from Malta

HMHS *Britannic* being escorted by tugs as she arrives at Southampton.

Imperial War Museum

was a passenger who the British would no doubt later regret having transported on that particular voyage.

Adalbert Franz Messany was a 24 year old Austrian opera singer who had been in Egypt when the war broke out in 1914. As an enemy national he was soon interned by the British and later transferred to Malta where he arrived on 1st December 1914.

After becoming ill with tuberculosis, the British authorities decided to repatriate him and he was placed on the *Wandilla* which sailed from Malta on 24th October and arrived at Mudros two days later. He was then transferred aboard the *Britannic* to be taken back to England for eventual repatriation to Austria.

While the *Britannic* was anchored at Mudros he was able to witness the transfer of the personnel and packages from the *Britannic* to the *Wandilla* and the other hospital ships while secured alongside. To further complicate matters, after two days confined in the mortuary he was placed in one of the wards where he continued to observe many of the activities on board during the voyage home.

After an interview with the Austrian authorities in Vienna on January 5th 1917, his observations were noted and later included in a German document published on 29th January 1917 listing 22 cases of alleged Allied abuses in the use and operation of hospital ships.

Loading completed, the *Britannic* left Mudros for the voyage home shortly after midday on 30th October, but once again the medical staff suffered another fatality when Corporal George Hunt of the R.A.M.C. died of dysentery and heart failure on 2nd November. He was buried at sea that evening.

Meanwhile as the remainder of the voyage continued uneventfully, Messany was able with few restrictions to speak freely to a number of fellow passengers. Included in this number were two soldiers in particular who would be mentioned by name in the German allegations as additional proof that the use of the *Britannic* as a hospital ship was being abused.

Messany stated that he had spoken to two British servicemen named Reg Taplay and Harold Hickman, alleging that Taplay had claimed to be a French translator

being transferred to France while Hickman claimed to be a German interpreter also being transferred to France. Neither made any mention of being ill and apparently also mentioned that there were 2,500 men on board who had been ordered to stay below decks and were fed different food from the hospital cases. When the ship reached Southampton on 6th November, Messany was able to observe these men on the quay as they were marched away in military formation though he did admit that they were not actually carrying any weapons. However, this was not true of the wounded officers in the wards who had been permitted to retain their side arms for the entire voyage. In his conversations with Hickman and Taplay, Messany admitted he was surprised that he had so few restrictions while on board and small wonder. On the face of it, it seems an incredible oversight by the authorities on board to allow Messany such freedom and enable him to make such potentially damaging observations.

After a month recuperating in Dartmouth Hospital, Messany was transferred to Holland for repatriation to Austria and he wasted no time in repeating what he had seen when questioned by the authorities. Once the Germans had published their accusations the Admiralty realised that every point would have to be disproved or justified if the neutrality of their hospital ships was to continue to be respected.

Taplay and Hickman were both traced and questioned about their alleged comments during the voyage. Taplay was actually a Private in the R.A.M.C. and was being repatriated suffering from dysentery. On arrival at Southampton he had been transferred to hospital in Manchester before being discharged to sick furlough on 7th March 1917. Hickman was a Private in the Welsh Hussars suffering from malaria. On return to England he had been sent to hospitals at Eastleigh and then Nottingham before being discharged to sick furlough just in time for Christmas on 19th December. Both denied ever claiming to be interpreters but as it was true that they could both speak a foreign language they did have an 'L' on their sleeves. Any soldier at Salonika with a foreign language had this distinguishing symbol on their uniform so during their conversations on board, Messany may have mis-understood what was said.

If the allegations against Taplay and Hickman had been disproved-in British eyes at least- there still remained the question of the 2,500 men who were ordered to remain out of sight whilst on board and marched away after the ship arrived in Southampton. A breakdown of the 3,022 invalids on board during the voyage showed that only 367 were actually 'cot cases', or in other words unable to leave their beds. The 'non cot cases' or walking wounded were certainly on different rations from those of the more seriously ill invalids on board whose diets varied from patient to patient, but they still needed constant attention from the medical orderlies on board nonetheless. There were also no restrictions to any of the men being allowed on deck as long as they were permitted by the senior medical officer and provided they wore the official hospital suits that were supplied when they arrived on board.

Left: Troops marching away from the hospital ship *Aquitania*, berthed in the Ocean Dock at Southampton. It was a scene similar to this that lead to German allegations that the use of the *Britannic* as a hospital ship by the British was being abused.
Imperial War Museum

Perhaps the one defence that was not entirely convincing was the fact that the officers had been allowed to retain their side arms. The British claimed that the conveyance of weapons belonging to wounded officers at one time was not thought to be in contravention of the Geneva Convention, but conveniently: '...it was under consideration'.

It would not be true to say that Messany's allegations had any effect on the ultimate fate of the *Britannic* as he was not actually repatriated until after the ship had been lost. The whole affair though was certainly a serious embarrassment to the Admiralty, largely because a foreign national of an enemy country had been allowed to move about a major British hospital ship with surprisingly little supervision.

After the *Britannic* had been sunk on her very next voyage, the British press were quick to accuse Germany of every sea-going atrocity that they could imagine. But if the German Government could not justify the sinking of a hospital ship in human terms, these allegations that the *Britannic* was not what she claimed to be could certainly help them in terms of damage limitation as they tried to wriggle off the proverbial hook.

On 31st January 1917 Germany announced the immediate introduction of unrestricted submarine warfare but despite the immediate breaking of diplomatic relations between America and Germany, America was not drawn into the war for another two and a half months.

By this time though, the White Star Line had already suffered its most massive blow of the war. The line was destined to lose twelve ships either owned or managed by them during the conflict, but the greatest individual loss to the line was to come before 1916 had drawn to a close.

After less than a year in service the *Britannic* was to become the largest individual loss to the British mercantile marine of the war.

A port side view of *Britannic*.   *Imperial War Museum*

Britannic at Mudros in October 1916, embarking wounded from the Belfast built hospital ship *Galeka* of the Union Steamship Company.
Imperial War Museum

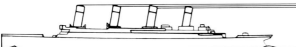

Chapter Six

Journey's End

With the diplomatic storm still to break, the bad weather that had accompanied the *Britannic* on her return to Southampton soon died down and the crew began to make their preparations for the return to the Mediterranean. Less than a week after returning, and in her fastest turnaround to date, the *Britannic* left Southampton for the last time at 2.23 pm on 12th November, once again bound for Mudros.

As the ship headed south on a calm but bitterly cold Sunday afternoon, the medical staff settled into their usual routine. The last voyage had been particularly successful, requiring no fewer than fifteen hospital trains to dispatch over three thousand wounded to the various medical depots throughout England and, with the on-board routine by now functioning smoothly, everyone was hoping for another successful and uneventful voyage.

The ship made steady progress, passing through the Straits of Gibraltar around midnight on the 15th, arriving at Naples on the morning of Friday 17th to take on coal and water as usual. By late afternoon the refuelling was completed and preparations were well underway to put to sea again when bad weather caught up with the ship once again. Any hopes of a quick departure were soon ended when the storm hit and for the next two days the *Britannic*

rode it out, secured by her three bow anchors and twenty hawsers fastening her stern to the wharf.

By Sunday afternoon the storm seemed to have broken and Captain Bartlett used the opportunity to put to sea. It turned out to be only a brief respite, however, and before he had dropped off the pilot the seas were beginning to rise once again. Fighting her way into the Bay of Naples, the *Britannic* immediately turned south. By the following morning the storms had died out and the ship was safely through the Straits of Messina, not that the medical staff on board would have much time to notice, for by this time they were in the final stages of preparing the ship for the thousands of wounded that would be coming aboard in the next 48 hours.

Indeed, there was much work to be done. The pack storesmen were busy issuing all manner of equipment and preparing for the mass of military kits that the wounded would bring with them, and Nurse Sheila Macbeth recorded that the nurses worked like factory hands from breakfast until their afternoon swim in the ship's pool. The intention was to complete the preparations early so that they would be able to enjoy a rest day before the patients came aboard, but while the nurses were enjoying their last taste of freedom before the *Britannic* arrived at Mudros, the clock was

HMHS *Britannic* at Mudros on 3rd October 1916.

National Maritime Museum

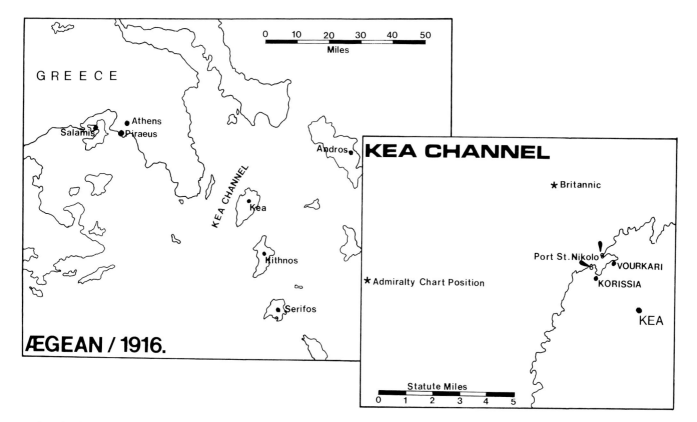

KEA CHANNEL

★ Britannic

Port St. Nikolo

VOURKARI

KORISSIA

★ Admiralty Chart Position

KEA

Statute Miles
0 1 2 3 4 5

GREECE

Athens
Salamis
Piraeus

Andros

KEA CHANNEL

Kea

Kithnos

Serifos

0 10 20 30 40 50
Miles

ÆGEAN / 1916.

already ticking as the last hours of the *Britannic*'s all too brief life ebbed away.

The seeds of the *Britannic*'s demise were actually sewn on 28th October 1916, the date that the ship had last arrived at Mudros. That same day the German submarine *U73* was lurking in the deep waters of the Kea Channel with a cargo of mines to off load and it is entirely possible that Kapitänleutnant Gustav Siess may even have observed his future victim. The log of the *U73* reports that hospital ships were sighted at 8.15 pm on the evening of October 27th and again at 3.25 am the following morning. Siess even placed his submarine in position for a torpedo attack on a "large steamer" heading in a north easterly direction

at 2.00 pm the same day, though the attack was aborted when the vessel was revealed to be a hospital ship. Could any of these vessels have been the *Britannic*?

Fortunately for the thousands of wounded aboard the *Britannic* the return journey had been uneventful, but while scouting the area Siess observed that all the vessels sailed along the Kea side of the strait. It was here that he chose to lay two mine barriers, each consisting of six mines, and it was into precisely these waters the *Britannic* now headed.

For the passengers and crew aboard the *Britannic* the last hours of the ship's life were completely normal. On the Monday evening the usual church service was held in the large dining saloon, described by Private Percy Tyler of

The German long range mine-laying submarine *U73*. Submarines of her type proved to be a great sucess but in operation were difficult to handle and in constant need of repair. She survived the war only to be scuttled by her own crew at Pola on 30th October 1918 after the Austrian surender.

National Maritime Museum

39

Major Harold Edgar Priestly R.A.M.C. Before joining the *Britannic*, Priestly was already famous for his work in the Wittenburg PoW Camp, being awarded the CMG in April 1916. *Angus Macbeth Mitchell/Sheila Macbeth Mitchell*

the R.A.M.C. as: "one of the best since the boat had been in commission". The last of the bad weather died out that evening as *Britannic* rounded Cape Matapan and by the morning of Tuesday 21st November the ship was off the Gulf of Athens and making twenty knots.

The journey to Mudros was almost over and everything on board was proceeding exactly according to the normal daily routine. Shortly before 8.00 am Captain Bartlett altered course to bring his ship into the Kea Channel with Chief Officer Robert Hume and Fourth Officer D. McTavish manning the bridge. As eight bells were sounded Lookout J. Murray relieved J. Conelly at the end of his watch, while in the dining room the nurses were sitting down to their last meal before the ship was due to arrive at Mudros. Stewardess Violet Jessop – who had not only survived the loss of the *Titanic* but had also been on board the *Olympic* during her collision with HMS *Hawke* – was in one of the galleys making up a breakfast tray for a sick nurse, and Sheila Macbeth was rushing into the dining room a few minutes late. Reverend John Fleming, also late for breakfast, was still in his cabin gazing out of the porthole at a distant island, while Percy Tyler and the other men of the R.A.M.C. had already eaten. Tyler was now sitting on his bunk in barrack room number 2 "industriously polishing his buttons". Nothing on board was at all unusual.

The normality was shattered at 8.12 am by the sound of a loud explosion that Reverend Fleming later described

as "...if a score of plate glass windows had been smashed together", Sheila Macbeth also remembering a great shudder that ran down the length of the ship. Before any of the nurses began to panic, Major Harold Priestly took command of the situation in the dining room and calmly instructed everyone to remain where they were and continue their breakfast as the Captain had not sounded the alarm.

Further aft the shock of the explosion was less apparent. Down in barrack room 2 Percy Tyler felt a violent bump which: "sent me forward a few paces and back again, then the boat regularly danced". Some men made casual remarks about having hit something while others said they were sorry for the boat that they had run into, but nobody seemed to take it seriously in that quarter of the ship. It was only when a man ran in five minutes later saying that the alarm had gone and that everyone was to get their life belts and go up on deck that the true seriousness of the situation became clear.

Up on the bridge, however, Charles Bartlett, only too aware of what had happened, was desperately trying to determine the best possible action to save his command. An explosion had occurred on the starboard side near the bulkhead between cargo holds 2 and 3, though with only two compartments open to the sea the ship should not have been in danger. But there was worse news to come. The ship's watertight skin only extended as far forward as boiler room 6, and the blast had not only destroyed the bulkhead between holds 2 and 3, but had also damaged the bulkhead between hold No. 1 and the forepeak. Incredibly, the bulkhead between hold No. 3 and boiler room 6 seemed to be intact, but the fireman's tunnel running between that boiler room and the firemen's quarters in the bow of the ship had been severely damaged and water was entering the boiler room through the open watertight door. With the *Britannic*'s situation deteriorating rapidly, Captain Bartlett ordered the watertight doors closed, a distress signal to be sent signalling that the *Britannic* had struck a mine off Port St. Nikolo and for the crew to uncover the boats.

The situation was undeniably serious, but the *Britannic* was designed to float with up to six of her forward compartments flooded and only four were actually open to the sea. Unfortunately, however, the watertight door between boiler rooms 5 and 6 had failed to close properly and this was allowing water to penetrate further aft. If the explosion had occurred at a time when the watch had not been changing then this door would very likely have been closed and the *Britannic* would probably have been able to remain afloat. In the end the damage was to prove quite fatal.

Nor was time on Captain Bartlett's side, for although the area of blast damage to the *Britannic* did not extend as far along the hull as the 250ft gash caused to the *Titanic* by the iceberg, internally the situation was far more serious. Four years earlier the pumps in boiler room 5 of the *Titanic* had contained the flooding until the water from boiler room 6 flowed over the dividing bulkhead. Now, on the *Britannic*, the open bulkhead doors meant that the two forward boiler rooms had to be evacuated barely two minutes after the blast. The bulkhead between boiler rooms 5 and 4 on the *Britannic*, however, was undamaged and extended up to the bridge deck (B deck) whereas on the *Titanic* it had only extended as high as E deck.

To further complicate matters, along with the damage to the bow and open watertight doors, the *Britannic* very quickly developed a serious list to starboard. Barely fifteen minutes after the explosion the portholes on E deck,

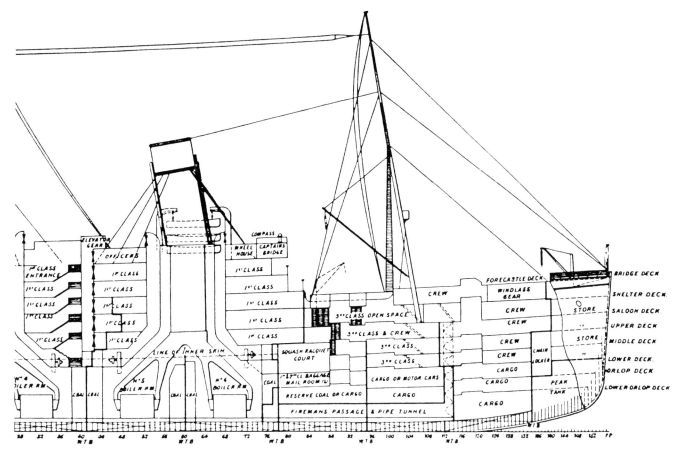

The explosion occured on the starboard side near the bulkhead betwen hold Nos. 2 and 3.

normally 25ft above the waterline, were beneath the surface. To make matters worse, many of them were open. They had been opened earlier that morning to ventilate the lower decks of the ship before the wounded were embarked later that day and the resulting inrush of water through the starboard portholes was to have a disastrous effect on the stability of the ship and could well have been a significant reason for the ship's loss. One thing of which we can be certain, however, is that open watertight doors and portholes in a war zone does indicate a somewhat cavalier attitude to a number of simple precautions that would, in all probability, have saved the ship.

Reverend John A. Fleming with a group of nurses. Fleming escaped from the sinking *Britannic* in the second to last lifeboat to be lowered from the starboard side.

Angus Macbeth Mitchell/Sheila Macbeth Mitchell

Assessing the options, Captain Bartlett decided that his best chance was to make a dash for the nearby island of Kea in an attempt to beach the ship, but this was easier said than done. The increasing list to starboard, combined with the weight of the 102 ton rudder, had impaired the steering gear and it was only with the help of the undamaged propellers that he was able to turn the ship and head towards the shore. Even then the forward momentum was something of a mixed blessing, for although the shoreline was gradually getting closer, the forward compartments began to fill more rapidly. Ordering the engines stopped, Captain Bartlett realised that the priority was to get everybody safely off before making any further attempt to save the ship. As the *Britannic* continued to settle rapidly by the bow, the order to lower the boats was given.

As the crew were struggling to save the ship, the nurses had nervously resumed their meal with an unnatural silence permeating the dining room. Reverend Fleming, meanwhile, had grabbed his life belt and immediately headed for his emergency station in one of the lower wards to make sure that no one needed any assistance, only to be greeted by the sight of empty beds that would not be occupied until after the *Britannic* had arrived at Mudros. As he headed for the dining room the alarm finally sounded and suddenly the passageway was filled the nurses filed out in an orderly manner. Returning to his cabin to fetch his coat and Bible, Fleming then headed for the relative safety of the boat deck.

As the evacuation of the *Britannic* progressed, help was already on the way. At 8.15 am the British destroyer *Scourge*, while arranging for the beached Greek steamer *Sparti* to be towed after having struck a mine off the island of Phleva the previous day, picked up Captain Bartlett's

SOS from Port St. Nikolo. Ordering the French tugs *Goliath*, *Polyphemus* and trawler No. 258 to follow, *Scourge*, under the command of Lieutenant Commander Henry Tupper, immediately set a course for the Kea Channel. Twenty minutes later the destroyer HMS *Foxhound* was also signalled by *Scourge* to break off from her patrol in the Gulf of Athens and proceed at once to the Kea Channel.

Luckily there was help even closer at hand. The auxiliary cruiser *Heroic*, under the command of Lieutenant Commander Percival Ram R.N.R., had passed the *Britannic* earlier that morning bound from Mudros to Salamis with mails. At 8.28 am she was just turning north into the Gulf of Athens when the *Britannic*'s distress signal was received. Ram immediately ordered the *Heroic*'s course reversed to go to the aid of the stricken hospital ship.

With help fast approaching, the evacuation continued in an orderly manner. Captain Harry Dyke, the assistant commander of the *Britannic*, was arranging the lowering of the boats from the aft davits on the starboard boat deck. As the nurses were being counted into the boats by ship's matron Mrs E. A. Dowse, a veteran of the Sudan and Boer Wars, their calm discipline as they awaited their turn on the promenade deck below was not mirrored by a group of firemen who had taken one of the boats from the poop deck without authority, even though it was filled to nowhere near its capacity. Rushing from his station, Dyke ordered them to pick up a number of men who had already jumped overboard before returning to his own davits to continue evacuating the women. It was only after all the nurses in her charge were accounted for that Mrs Dowse finally stepped into one of the boats herself, becoming a real heroine of the sinking as opposed to the "sixty year old dug out" described in her autobiography *A Testament of Youth* by Vera Brittain who had been one of the V.A.D. personnel transported to Malta two voyages earlier.

Fifth Officer G. Fielding was also busy. After swinging out two boats on the port gantry davits it was all he could do to stop a group of seamen and stewards from rushing the boats. He managed to persuade the seamen to return to their stations but, realising that he would probably be better off with the stewards out of the way, he proceeded to lower the boats to within six feet of the water. With the *Britannic* still underway, however, he held back from releasing them until the ship had come to a complete halt, much to the annoyance of the occupants.

Fielding's precautions were to prove more than justified because it was at about this time that the great tragedy of the day occurred. Variations in the details from the eyewitnesses to the horrific events that were to follow mean we will probably never know exactly what went wrong, but bearing in mind the famous inward pull of the Olympic class liners it is not difficult to understand what occurred. Just as the suction of the turning screws had caused the cruiser HMS *Hawke* to ram the *Olympic* in September 1911 and the liner *New York* to be pulled from her moorings at Southampton as the *Titanic* passed her by in April 1912, so two of *Britannic*'s port lifeboats that had been lowered without authority and tiny by comparison were drawn in. The occupants had no chance and the boats were dashed to pieces by the 23ft propellers which were by this time breaking the surface. One of the more fortunate survivors was Violet Jessop who, along with the other occupants of

Captain Harry William Dyke (*left*) born in 1869, served on the *Olympic* from March 1913 before being appointed as *Britannic*'s Assistant Captain in December 1915. Curiously, details of his career following the loss of the *Britannic* until his death in 1927 are obscure. *Harold Roberts*

Below: The aft port davits where Captain Dyke was stationed as the ship sank. The davits did little to enhance the *Britannic*'s profile, but they did free a great deal of space on the boat deck. *Angus Macbeth Mitchell/Sheila Macbeth Mitchell*

The auxiliary cruiser HMS *Heroic* was the nearest British ship to hear the distress call from the *Britannic* and succeeded in rescuing 494 survivors.

National Maritime Museum

her boat, had seen what was about to happen and jumped overboard in an attempt to escape. As she jumped into the water she was pulled under by the suction and spun around by the propeller. When she finally came to the surface she hit her head on the keel of the lifeboat but, as luck would have it, she was clear of the ship and quickly pulled to safety. It might have been worse but word of the incident reached the bridge and the engines were stopped before a third boat was also pulled in. As the propellers came to a halt Captain T. Fernhead of the R.A.M.C. and two other men were able to push against the now motionless propeller blade until the boat was clear, but by then more than seventy people had been either killed or horribly injured.

Despite a lack of experienced oarsmen, as soon as it was safe the undamaged lifeboats manoeuvred to where survivors were floating in the water. Once the survivors had been dragged aboard nurses tore up their aprons and even life belts to serve as temporary bandages, while the boats moved clear of the stern to avoid being caught in the suction when the ship finally sank.

It was at about 8.35 am that Captain Bartlett gave the official order to abandon ship and almost immediately the forward set of port side gantry davits became inoperable. Luckily the aft set was still functioning and Fielding was able to launch another three boats in quick succession.

One of the boats launched was commanded by First Officer H. Hollingsworth who would have more reason than most to appreciate the seriousness of the situation. Hollingsworth had been ordered to take a boat and arrange the rescue of the many swimmers in the water, and having nearly drowned when the White Star liner *Arabic* was torpedoed by the *U24* in August 1915 his anxiety was perfectly understandable. The *Arabic* went down in barely eleven minutes with the loss of 44 lives, so the seriousness of the situation now facing the *Britannic* was not lost on her First Officer.

Within ten minutes of the order to abandon ship the increasing list to starboard made any further use of the port davits impossible, and the davit crews moved to the central island on the boat deck to throw deck chairs and life rafts to the swimmers below. Fielding was even considering that one of these rafts would probably save

his own life when he noticed Sixth Officer J. Chapman struggling with one of the smaller boats serviced by the Welin davits. He then helped to manhandle the boat into position and lower it into the water, before escaping himself by slithering down the boat falls.

By now the end was near, yet despite the worsening situation men continued to go below. Percy Tyler made several trips to fetch life belts for those who didn't have them before helping to place one of the sea scouts "rather forcibly" into a lifeboat. Tyler himself was ordered into the same boat, the third last to be lowered.

Reverend Fleming's escape was also something of a last minute affair. He too had made a number of trips below to collect bread before helping to throw the deck chairs and life rafts over the side. He was finally ordered into the second last boat to leave by Major Priestly who, declining a seat himself, went to have a last look around to make sure that everyone was safe. Priestly himself escaped a few minutes later in the last boat to be lowered, along with Claude Lancaster, the *Britannic*'s purser, carrying the ship's log and papers with him.

To Captain Bartlett on the bridge it was obvious that the end was not far off. As the waters steadily rose up over the bow and the *Britannic* continued to heel over onto her starboard side, he sounded one final blast on the ship's whistle signalling the order to abandon ship. He then simply walked off the starboard wing of the bridge and into the water. This was a timely signal for Chief Engineer Robert Fleming and the remaining engineers who, like their counterparts on the *Titanic*, remained at their posts until the last possible minute. They escaped via the only possible route left to them; up the staircase and through the funnel casing of the fourth smoke stack which acted as a ventilator for the reciprocating engine room.

As the ship continued to heel over, one by one the funnels gave way under the strain. Observers in the lifeboats, keeping their distance as the ship went down, could only watch and listen to the boilers inside the hull exploding as the water poured into the open funnel casings. The ship finally rolled over to starboard with the stern slipping below the surface at 9.07 am, leaving 35 lifeboats and hundreds of survivors in the water scattered over a large area.

The *Britannic* had sunk in less than an hour, though her end had mercifully been less tragic than it might have been. Had her wards been filled with wounded soldiers then the loss of life could have been catastrophic. As it was, casualties were minimal when the explosion occurred; almost everyone on board had been away from the area of the blast having their breakfast. Indeed, if it had not been for the accident to the two lifeboats, it's entirely possible that there would have been scarcely any casualties at all.

There were still wounded, however, who needed attention. Captain Bartlett swam to a collapsible boat floating nearby and from there began to co-ordinate the rescue of survivors floating in the water. The smoke of the approaching rescue ships could already be seen on the horizon so, while the lifeboats continued to pick up the survivors, he ordered the motor launches to collect the wounded and make for Port St. Nikolo.

Actually, help was even closer at hand. Francesco Psilas, a fisherman from St. Nikolo, was very quickly on the scene and pulled several men from the water. In recognition of his services the Admiralty later paid him £4 through the British Consul at Syra. But the British were not far away. At 10.00 am the *Scourge* sighted lifeboats floating in the distance and ten minutes later her engines were stopped as boats were lowered to help pick up survivors. A few minutes earlier the *Heroic* had also lowered her boats, barely an hour after the *Britannic* had sunk.

Meanwhile, all that remained of the largest British steamer of her day were 35 lifeboats scattered around the Kea Channel amongst a sea of survivors, flotsam and assorted wreckage. In less than one hour a single weapon had once more shattered the myth of the unsinkable ship and White Star's plans for a trio of super liners on the North Atlantic.

The British G class destroyers *Foxhound* (*below*) and *Scourge* (*right*) were also quick to respond to the distress call. The G class destroyers were the last British destroyers to be built that were coal fired and were scrapped soon after the war.
National Maritime Museum

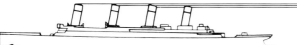

Chapter Seven

Casualties Of War

After two hours searching through the wreckage, the *Heroic* had picked up some 494 survivors and space was fast running out. On board the *Scourge* things were little better, with 339 other survivors filling most of the 270 ft of available deck space and there were at least another 150 still in Port St. Nikolo, many badly injured.

The situation was saved by the arrival of HMS *Foxhound* at 11.45 am, under the command of Lieutenant Commander William Shuttleworth. The light cruiser HMS *Foresight* and the auxiliary cruiser HMS *Chasseur* were also fast approaching so Commander Tupper decided that they had done as much as possible. After advising Shuttleworth that there were still survivors on Kea, *Heroic* and *Scourge* set a course for Piraeus just before midday.

After sweeping the area for any remaining survivors, *Foxhound* dropped anchor in Port St. Nikolo at 1.00 pm and immediately arranged with Captain Bartlett to have the wounded taken on board. Within an hour HMS *Foresight*

was also anchored in the harbour and, after sending medical officers to assist with the casualties, offered to take the wounded to Mudros. However, with the survivors by now on board *Foxhound*, Shuttleworth decided that it would save time and trouble if they were taken directly to Piraeus as he had been instructed. *Foxhound* duly weighed anchor at 2.15 pm. *Foresight*, meanwhile, remained behind to see to the remaining lifeboats and to arrange for the burial on the island of Sergeant W. Sharpe, who had died of his injuries.

As the rescue ships turned north into the Gulf of Athens, some of the wounded succumbed to their injuries. On board the *Heroic* Private A. W. Binks and Fireman C. Phillips died from the injuries they received when their lifeboat was destroyed by the ship's propellers, while Fireman J. Brown died on board the French tug *Goliath*, having failed to recover after being pulled from the water unconscious. *Scourge* and *Foxhound* completed the journey without loss of life. In all, a total of 30 men had failed to

Surviving crew members of the *Britannic* on the deck of the British battleship HMS *Lord Nelson* at Salonika awaiting transportation back to England.

Imperial War Museum

Above: The 14,000 ton British pre-*Dreadnought* HMS *Duncan*, flagship of the British Adriatic Fleet, was the venue for the investigation into the loss of the *Britannic*. Already an ageing and outdated vessel, *Duncan* was withdrawn from service at the end of the war. *National Maritime Museum*

survive the ordeal, but stories of incredible escapes testified to how much worse it could have been.

Most amazing of all was that, despite the scale of the damage, because everybody was either at breakfast or changing watch at the time nobody was killed in the explosion. There were still a number of close calls, however. In his report to the medical authorities on Malta, Colonel Anderson noted that Private John Cuthbertson, the only person in the forward barrack room on G deck, was able to get clear even though the staircase had been blown away and the room quickly flooded. In fact Cuthbertson's escape owed far more to luck than judgement, with Percy Tyler recalling that he was in fact washed from the ward on G deck all the way up to E deck by the force of the water. As it turned out, the situation there wasn't much better; another man in one of the forward lavatories on E deck reported that the steward's and scout's quarters were completely wrecked in the blast. He was only just able to stumble over the wreckage and get clear before the area was awash.

Then there were tales of heroism: the engineers remaining at their post until the last signal to abandon ship; Lieutenant John Cropper giving his life belt to someone who had lost their own only to perish himself; Sea Scout Edward Ireland having to be carried from the bridge and forcibly placed in a lifeboat; Captain E. G. Fenton deliberately lowering himself into the water by a dangling rope because he knew from a previous shipwreck experience that as he was so large he would occupy the space of two

men in a lifeboat; Lieutenant J. Starkie dashing below to get food for those in the boats and only escaping himself by swimming off the boat deck after the bridge was already submerged. Then there was Major Priestly, who only escaped in the last boat after doing all in his power to make sure that everyone was safe. Priestly himself later downplayed his role in the disaster, saying that it was "a mere picnic" compared with his experiences in the Wittenberg prisoner of war camp, but his modesty did not prevent Colonel Anderson from specifically mentioning him in his dispatch.

The tales of heroism and good fortune, however, were of secondary importance to the more pressing business of the immediate tending to the wounded and housing of over one thousand survivors. At 3.45 pm *Heroic* arrived in the Bay of Salamis alongside HMS *Duncan*, the flagship of the Royal Navy's Adriatic Squadron, and for the next three hours the distribution of over one thousand survivors, some badly injured, continued as rapidly as possible.

The task of tending to the injured fell to Fleet Surgeon Nelson Roche aboard HMS *Duncan*, and it didn't take long for the shortage of space to make itself apparent. By the time *Foxhound* arrived alongside at 5.30 pm, *Duncan*'s sick bay was already full to overflowing, so as soon as the uninjured survivors had been taken off, *Foxhound* proceeded to Piraeus. By 8.00 pm she was secured alongside a grain wharf which was serving as a military pier and the injured were being taken off for transfer to the nearby Russian Hospital.

The real problem lay in what to do with the uninjured survivors. The logistics involved in clothing, housing and feeding over one thousand unexpected personnel were daunting enough, though Admiral Arthur Hayes-Sadler's dilemma was considerably eased by the timely intervention of Admiral Darrieus, the commander of the French Third Squadron, who immediately placed his ships at Hayes-Sadler's disposal. As soon as the *Heroic* and *Scourge* had transferred all their wounded aboard the *Duncan*, boats sent out from the French ships began to disperse the uninjured survivors around the fleet.

Captain Bartlett and the other senior personnel, whose presence would be necessary for the enquiry, remained aboard HMS *Duncan*, while each French warship took aboard some 70 survivors. Of the remaining ship's crew and medical orderlies, three hundred were transferred to the ex-Greek depot ship *Kanaris*, while a few officers and men were quartered on board the steamer *Marienbad*. With no space left, the remaining officers along with the nurses and stewardesses, were taken ashore at 6.00 pm for transfer to hotels at Phaleron.

With the survivors taken care of, activity at Piraeus began to return to something like normal. At 7.25 pm a launch from the flagship arrived alongside *Heroic* to collect the bodies of Binks and Phillips, having already retrieved that of Fireman J. Brown from Piraeus. *Scourge* weighed anchor at 7.40 pm and shortly after midnight *Foxhound* also left to return to her patrol line. The following morning both vessels were back in the Kea Channel sweeping for mines.

While the British port control officer at Piraeus,

Nurse Sheila Macbeth at the Russian Hospital. The Greek doctors seemed to resent the presence of British nurses but because Sheila spoke a little French she became indispensable. Following the sinking she would much rather have stayed in Greece than return to a home hospital, but in the end she was shipped home with the other nurses, arriving back in England on Boxing Day 1916.
Angus Macbeth Mitchell/Sheila Macbeth Mitchell

Always. Merry and Bright.

Saved from "Britannic" wreck on Nov. 20, 1916.

L.H. Lewes. X WARD. HMHS Britannic Nov. 4R. 1916.

This caricature by one of the *Britannic*'s patients shows that even in war time the wounded were able to retain a sense of humour. *Paul Louden Brown Collection*

Lieutenant W. H. Rogers, arranged for the accommodation and transport of the survivors, including a car for the matron and nurses between the Hotel Aktaion at Phaleron and the Russian Hospital at Piraeus, the task of conducting the enquiry fell to Captain Hugh Heard, the commanding officer of the *Duncan*, and his chief engineer, Commander George Staer.

The reasons for the ship's loss had to be examined as quickly and as completely as possible, though the thoroughness of the investigation into the loss of the *Britannic* would fall a long way short of that carried out by Lord Mersey at the *Titanic* enquiry four years earlier. Mersey's enquiry enjoyed the benefit of virtually unlimited resources and time, whereas the *Britannic*'s survivors were scattered around the fleet and liable to be shipped home at any time.

While Heard and Staer busied themselves with their report, arrangements were made for the burial of the dead. At 1.20 pm on 22nd November, the ensign on the *Duncan* was lowered to half mast while the bodies of Binks, Phillips and Brown were taken ashore by the funeral detail, complete

The nurses outside the Aktaion Hotel in Athens. Fortunately the hotel was closed for the winter so there was plenty of space available, though at first many had difficulty finding a bed because the hotel had prepared rooms for eighteen instead of eighty.
Angus Macbeth Mitchell/Sheila Macbeth Mitchell

with firing party. The procession to the graveyard included representatives not only from the British and French Fleets, but also many local Greek dignitaries, sympathisers and British residents who had sent wreaths and condolences. That afternoon, Binks, Phillips and Brown were buried in the graveyard at Piraeus with full military honours.

As the funeral services were taking place, the crew of the *Duncan* still had their normal duties to attend to. These were not made any easier by the congestion of the *Britannic*'s salvaged lifeboats in the waters around the flagship. When another four boats were returned from the French ship *Verité* at 4.00 pm, orders were finally given for the lifeboats to be transferred to the Salamis dockyard over the next several days.

For Charles Bartlett there was little he could do now except assist the enquiry and confirm the number of casualties of the sinking. Slowly a more complete picture began to emerge as the lists of who had survived or been injured were completed, and on 24th November Captain Bartlett was finally able to record in the log that 21 members of the *Britannic*'s crew had been killed. A further nine officers and men of the R.A.M.C. were added to the list, bringing the final total of those killed to 30.

Of the 1,036 survivors there were 45 wounded. The last fatality, Lookout H. Honeycutt, had reached Piraeus alive only to die at the Russian hospital, but of the remaining casualties there would be no need to record any further loss. When Reverend Fleming visited them in hospital the only complaint he heard was that the local food "wasn't equal to their appetites".

By 24th November Heard and Staer had collected as much evidence as they felt was possible under the circumstances and they submitted their report to Hayes-Sadler. The report itself was quick to accept its own shortcomings, which were largely due to the difficulty of finding so many witnesses scattered around the fleet and the lack of time available to interview them. The picture that had emerged, however, did seem to be the most likely.

Despite claims that there had been more than one explosion, Heard and Staer concluded that the most reliable evidence indicated that there had in fact been only one, but conflicting stories from several of the witnesses meant that the actual cause was by no means certain.

The possibility that the *Britannic* had been deliberately torpedoed was supported by a statement from Steward P. Walters, in which he reported seeing the track of an approaching torpedo on the port side. As he had at one time served as an officer's steward in the Royal Navy and had witnessed torpedo exercises at sea, clearly his evidence could not be brushed aside lightly. Walters was so sure of what he had seen that he even clutched the rails to avoid being knocked over by the explosion, though he did admit to not actually having seen the torpedo itself. The torpedo theory was given a further boost by the testimony of H. Etches, one of the ship's bakers, who had been on another part of the deck at the time. An important difference in the two men's testimonies, however, was that although they both claimed to have seen the track of a torpedo, Walters claimed it had been on the port side, while Etches' torpedo had been aft and to starboard. Nevertheless, the confirmation that a torpedo had sunk the *Britannic* would have suited many at the War Office in London, providing yet another indication of the depths to which the Germans would stoop. Not content with the murder of innocent civilians on unarmed passenger liners, it seemed that they were now taking to deliberately sinking hospital ships specifically protected under the Geneva Convention.

Unfortunately it wasn't that straight forward. In his book *The Last Voyage of His Majesty's Hospital Ship Britannic*, Reverend Fleming stated that shortly before 8.00 am on the morning of the sinking "moving objects resembling barrels" had been reported. This in itself is particularly odd because German mines were normally to be found anything between two and six metres beneath the surface, while the Kea Channel had been swept for mines a few days earlier. Accounts from the inhabitants of Port St. Nikolo that a submarine had been sighted earlier that morning some time before the explosion indicated that mines could well have been laid in the area since the channel had been swept, but then again it could also add to the credibility of the torpedo theory.

No doubt Walters and Etches were genuinely convinced that they had seen a torpedo but, as their statements failed to agree upon which side it had been observed, the evidence was hardly conclusive. Heard also noted that, when the explosion had occurred, there was no report of any column of water being thrown up as was usual with torpedoes.

After nine paragraphs summarising the layout of the ship, the nature of the damage sustained and a number of possible reasons for the loss of the vessel – including the failure of the watertight doors in the forward part of the ship and the open scuttles on E deck – the final line of the report more or less exonerated the Germans from the deliberate sinking of the *Britannic*, stating: "The effects of

the explosion might have been due to either a mine or a torpedo. The probability seems to be a mine."

Admiral Hayes-Sadler added the report to the dispatches he had completed the previous day praising the conduct of the commanding officers of the *Heroic*, *Scourge* and *Foxhound*, and acknowledging the help from local fishermen and the French Consular Agents on Kea. He also recorded his gratitude to Admiral Darrieus and the officers and men of the French Fleet, before forwarding the two reports to Admiral Cecil Thursby at Salonika, the Senior Naval Officer in the Eastern Mediterranean.

The loss of the *Britannic* was having a far more serious impact on the war in the Aegean than simply a mass of extra paperwork. *Britannic* had been due at Mudros to transport some three thousand invalids back to England in order to ease the pressure on the already over stretched local medical facilities. These men still had to be evacuated to England in other ships before the hospitals at Mudros were overwhelmed.

To relieve the situation the smaller hospital ships *Warilda*, *Herefordshire*, *Wandilla*, *Llandovery Castle*, *Dover Castle* and *Glenart Castle* were ordered to return to England immediately with as many casualties as they could carry. Although this certainly relieved the immediate pressure on the hospitals, the diversion of these six ships, combined with the mining of the hospital ship *Braemar Castle* in the Mykoni Channel on 23rd November, placed an enormous strain on the remaining hospital ships.

Aquitania left on her next voyage to the Mediterranean before the end of November, by which time the Admiralty were fully aware of the hazardous situation in the Aegean. Unwilling to risk their only remaining giant hospital ship, Augusta once again became the new base for the transfer of wounded.

While the military authorities tried to sort out the mess in the Aegean, the loss of the *Britannic* was eventually announced in the press on 23rd November. The resulting outcry was predictable to say the least.

The Times was one of the more collected of the papers, simply reporting the Admiralty statement listing 1,106 survivors and estimating about 50 killed. The opportunity for valuable propaganda was not missed, however, and their Athens correspondent was quick to suggest that the ship may have been deliberately torpedoed, noting: "This new act of German barbarity excites profound indignation."

An over imaginative correspondent for *The Daily Mirror* went all out for maximum propaganda value, claiming: "...every effort was made to save over one thousand sick and wounded", conveniently overlooking the fact that there were no wounded on board at the time. The "error" was corrected in the following morning's edition, but by then the point had been well and truly made.

For the inhabitants of Southampton the sinking was brought closer to home when the newspapers published the list of casualties and those still missing. Among the list of dead were eleven crew members who came from in or around the town. The *Southampton Times* noted that one of the casualties, Fireman J. McFeat, also played football for the Southampton reserve team.

By Friday 24th November the stories in the papers had settled down. The reports that the ship had been carrying large numbers of wounded at the time of the sinking had been dropped, but speculation about the cause of the sinking continued unabated. The naval correspondent of *The Times* had no doubt what he thought, observing: "...a deliberate opportunity was made by the Germans to exhibit their

Vice Admiral Cecil Thursby, commander of the British naval forces in the Eastern Mediterranean. He accepted the report into the loss of the *Britannic* and forwarded the details to the Admiralty.   *Imperial War Museum*

The hospital ship *Braemar Castle* struck a mine in the Mykoni Channel two days after the *Britannic* was sunk. She was sucessfully beached and later returned to service.

Imperial War Museum

disregard for the laws of nations and at the same time to get rid of a vessel likely to be a formidable competitor for passenger traffic after the war." The German authorities, of course, did their utmost to counter the British claims and at the same time plant suspicion in the minds of neutral America that the ship may not have been all that she seemed. A communiqué from Berlin published in *The Times* claimed:

"According to reports so far at hand, the ship was on its way from England to Salonika. For a journey in this direction the large number of persons on board is extraordinarily striking, which justifies the forcible suspicion of the misuse of the hospital ship for purposes of transport. Inasmuch as the ship carried distinguishing marks of a hospital ship, in accordance with regulations, there can naturally be no question of a German submarine in connection with the sinking."

In fact the Germans were skating on thin ice in claiming that a clearly marked hospital ship would not be deliberately torpedoed. In February 1915 the hospital ship *Asturias* had been attacked in just such a manner in the English Channel, though on that occasion the ship had taken evasive action and the torpedo had missed it's mark. Two years later the *Asturias* would not be so lucky, but the fact remained that the markings of a hospital ship were not always a suitable deterrent to a particularly zealous U-boat captain.

The first real indication of the reason for the loss of the *Britannic* came a few months before the end of the war. After the *UB109* had been sunk off Dover in August 1918,

one of the interrogated prisoners claimed that he had been on board the *U73* in 1916 and that the submarine had laid mines in the Kea Channel less than an hour before the *Britannic* had reached the area. The story was partially confirmed in German newspapers after the war by Gustav Siess, who had commanded the *U73* from October 1915 to April 1917. In what turned out to be a particularly successful voyage, it was confirmed that mines from the *U73* not only accounted for the damage to the *Braemar Castle*, but also for the sinking of the 12,481 ton French steamer *Burdigala* off the island of Mikonos, barely a week before the *Britannic* was also sunk.

To counter the German claims, the Admiralty published in the same edition of *The Times* their justification for so many people being on board. Of the 1,125 listed as on board at the time, 625 were members of the ship's crew while the remaining 500 were described as medical staff, consisting of 25 officers (R.A.M.C), 76 nurses and 399 medical orderlies, lab attendants and clerical staff. One can only wonder what the Germans would have made of the figures if the *Britannic* had been sunk on her previous voyage when she had in fact been transporting nearly 500 other medical staff to foreign stations.

As the allegations and denials flew back and forth, the issue of the *Britannic* was overshadowed by the death of Franz Josef I on the evening of the same day that the *Britannic* had gone to the bottom. The death of the one man really capable of holding the Austro-Hungarian Empire together suddenly made everything else pale into insignificance.

Nor did the loss of the *Britannic* have the same effect on the American public as the attacks on the *Lusitania* and *Arabic*. These two vessels had been deliberately torpedoed and innocent civilians had died, whereas the *Britannic* was a serving hospital ship and had in all probability been sunk by a less discriminating mine rather than deliberately targeted. Had the ship been sunk on the return voyage from Mudros to Southampton, the casualty lists could have exceeded those of the *Lusitania* and *Titanic* combined and the American response might have been very different.

To the survivors, however, their most immediate priority was to get safely back to England, though the journey home would be a far cry from the relative comfort to which they had become accustomed aboard the *Britannic*.

On 24th November the *Britannic*'s officers and uninjured crew were transferred aboard the RFA *Ermine* for transportation to Salonika via the Makronisos Channel. The journey took the better part of two days, and having already been shipwrecked once in the last week, the fact that the *Ermine* carried only four lifeboats was lost on most of the 605 survivors crammed on board. *Ermine* finally arrived at Salonika shortly before midnight on 26th November and the following morning the survivors were given their first proper meal in days and the chance for a quick bath aboard HMS *Nelson* before boarding the transport *Royal George*.

The *Royal George* left Salonika at 3.30 pm on November 27th. Thus far the journey had, all things considered, been relatively comfortable, but things were to change radically when the ship reached Marseilles on December 2nd. Here Captain Bartlett finally parted from his crew, taking a scheduled passenger train, but for the other men it was the beginning of a four day ordeal. Leaving Marseilles a little after 5.30 pm on 4th December, they were packed into unheated carriages, while outside it was snowing heavily. Brief stops at Louvre, Lyon, Macon, Dijon and Nantes offered little in the way of refreshment other than the occasional mug of black tea. At Louvre the hungry crew rushed the carriage containing the rations of bully beef and biscuits, and virtually fought for the food. The officers managed to find a passable meal at a local hotel but other than that the refreshments were basic to say the least. A one hour stop at Nantes provided the opportunity for a quick wash, but the water was ice cold and the only way to keep warm in the freezing weather was to go for a run around the station.

The 50 hour train journey finally ended when the train pulled in to the station at Le Havre shortly after 8 pm on 6th December. It was then a five mile march to the camp followed by another freezing night, this time on bare wooden boards under canvas without even a blanket. For many sleep was impossible and they got through the night only by running around the camp in an attempt to keep warm. The following morning, however, the men did receive a meagre breakfast, though once again the officers were able to get to a nearby village for a quick clean up. Following a meal of hot stew and bread, that afternoon the men completed a six mile march to Le Havre, and on 7th December they finally embarked on the transport *Caesarea*. By this time a number of the men were so weak that they fainted, one even falling into the dock, but at least *Caesarea* provided the first real warmth and comfortable bunks that the men had known in nearly a week.

Arriving back at Southampton at 9.00 am the following day, for some the privations of the journey were considerably offset when Captain Bartlett greeted them with the joyous news that, due to their conduct on the day of the sinking, any fines previously imposed had been cancelled and that they would also be granted the usual two weeks survivor's leave.

For most of the medical staff the journey home wasn't much different. Along with the wounded, they were transferred aboard the hospital ship *Grantully Castle* at Piraeus on 27th November for transportation to Malta and eventual repatriation to England via troop transports to Marseilles. To be spared the discomfort and hardships of the overland route, the nurses were held in Malta until the hospital ship *Valdivia* was available to transport them in relative safety to England. They arrived back at Southampton on 26th December, but the men had to suffer the same route as the *Britannic*'s crew two weeks earlier.

Percy Tyler's journal of his journey home reads much the same as the description of the crew's journey. After ten days on Malta, on the morning of 10th December the men of the R.A.M.C. boarded the transport *Huntsend* bound for Marseilles, but due to stormy weather and the zigzag course the ship took six days to arrive at her destination. The monotony of the voyage was only broken by the band of HMT *Minnewaska* who were also being repatriated because their ship too had come to grief on mine near Mudros barely a week after the *Britannic* went down. Once at Marseilles the same nightmare train journey to Le Havre ensued, with nine men packed into compartments of a little under 40ft square, surviving on meagre rations, black tea and cigarettes.

Reaching Le Havre in the early hours of 20th December, it was not until that evening that Tyler boarded the transport *King Edward*, finally arriving at Southampton at 10.30 the following morning, an entire month after the *Britannic* had met her fate.

The nightmare was over. The crew and medical staff would duly be reassigned to other vessels or theatres of war after their survivor's leave, but for the White Star Line it was business as usual. On 18th December, Henry Concanon closed the *Britannic*'s registry at Liverpool and the ship officially ceased to exist. While the great hospital ship was no more, there was still a great deal of paperwork to be completed before the White Star Line could close their file on the lost ship.

The 2,850 ton British light cruiser HMS *Foresight* arrived too late to assist in the rescue of the survivors but still managed to anchor in Port St Nikolo and give medical assistance.
Imperial War Museum

The hospital ship *Grantully Castle* (Union-Castle Line) transported the surviving medical staff from Athens to Malta.
Imperial War Museum

The fleet auxiliary vessel RFA *Ermine* (*below*) transported the surviving crew members to Salonika before transferring them aboard the transport vessel *Royal George* (*left*) for transportation to Marseilles followed by an exhausting 50 hour train journey to Le Havre.
Imperial War Museum

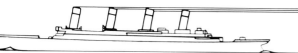

Chapter Eight
Picking Up The Pieces

The loss of the *Britannic* was a major blow for the White Star Line. When Joseph Bruce Ismay and William Pirrie had first envisaged White Star's trio of giant ships at their dinner party nearly ten years earlier, neither could have foreseen that only one of the three would ever complete a single commercial voyage between Southampton and New York.

The moment the *Britannic* disappeared beneath the surface at 9.07 am on Tuesday 21st November 1916, White Star's ambition to dominate the North Atlantic passenger routes between Europe and America seemed over, for the time being at least.

The loss of the *Titanic* in 1912 had been the first major blow, yet even though public confidence in the *Olympic* had been restored following her reconstruction in the winter of 1912-13, there was little hope of running a balanced service without a suitable running mate. The loss of the *Oceanic* in September 1914 further complicated the situation for it eliminated the only remaining ship in the fleet that came anywhere near to matching the *Olympic* in terms of speed and accommodation. The *Britannic*'s entry into service would have restored the situation, while plans for a fourth vessel – tentatively to be named *Germanic* but tactfully changed to *Homeric* following the outbreak of hostilities – were also at an advanced stage. Fate, however, was to intervene once more in the destiny of White Star Line.

In the space of a little over four and a half years White Star had lost three of their largest ships, and the demands of the war effort meant that the construction of ocean liners was a long way down on the list of national priorities. Even when replacement was possible, the lack of raw materials and soaring costs could only result in a huge strain on the company's resources; the *Titanic* and *Britannic* alone accounted for some £3,500,000 at pre-war prices. But all that was well in the future and there would be other casualties before the war had been won.

The *Britannic* was the fifth vessel that White Star had lost since the war had started, and the *Georgic* and *Russian* would also become casualties before 1916 was out. By the time the war was over, the White Star Line was to lose twelve ships either owned or operated by the company, amounting to a gross tonnage of over 200,000 tons.

Despite the gloomy outlook, at least White Star could take comfort in the fact that the company would not have to bear the entire cost of the reconstruction programme alone. The *Britannic* had gone down while in the service of the Admiralty and by that stage of the war the Government were assuming the majority of the insurance costs for vessels in their service. The White Star Line was due for a large pay out, but the problem was how to get the money?

By the end of May 1917 the final payments for the loss of the liners *Britannic*, *Laurentic* and *Afric* whilst in government service had still not been fully met. To be fair to the Admiralty, in the case of the *Britannic* full payment had not been made partly because the final calculations of the first cost of the vessel were not completed by Harland and Wolff until the second week of March 1917. The Admiralty had advanced £1,750,000 to White Star on 23rd January 1917 until the final accounts could be completed, but by the end of May no further payments had been received. Along with the outstanding payments following the loss of the *Laurentic* and *Afric*, the Admiralty still owed over £600,000 to the White Star Line alone, not to mention the other shipping lines with equally valid claims. Harold Sanderson's letter to the Admiralty on 31st May pressing for the settlement of the outstanding compensation was greeted with the customary stonewalling, though the Admiralty did at least agree to advance a further £100,000 to the company in mid-June.

Despite the magnitude of the disaster which had overwhelmed both the *Britannic* and the White Star Line, the small cogs of bureaucracy still turned up the odd little discrepancy of little or no consequence to the overall picture: in this case it was the White Star Line who found that a Steinway piano, originally intended for the *Britannic*, was still held by the contractors, Smith & Son. The cost of the piano had accidentally been included in the accounts sent to the Admiralty so White Star offered to buy it back for £45, unless the Admiralty had any use for it. Just how essential this piano was to the war effort will never be known as no trace can be found of the reply.

By the end of 1916 the situation in the Mediterranean had once again settled down, so much so that it proved possible to lay up the *Aquitania* once again. This time, however, the War Office heeded the advice of the Transport Division and she remained laid up at half rate throughout the whole of 1917 with the hospital fittings still on board. As 1917 moved on and the war followed it's course, Reverend Fleming's fears that the memory of the *Britannic* would soon fade away began to come true. Although the *Britannic* was larger than either of her sisters, to the public of 1917 she was just one of many fine ships to be sacrificed in the conflict, and with shipping losses reaching new heights following the German re-introduction of unrestricted submarine warfare (900,000 tons in April 1917 alone), somehow the memory of the *Britannic* was bound to be affected.

Despite the terrible losses of April 1917, however, the month also marked an important turning point in the war: the United States finally came in on the side of the Allies. Within months the Admiralty took the long overdue decision to adopt the convoy system and losses dropped dramatically. For the German Kaiser who had done so much to build up the German merchant and naval fleets it was the beginning of the end. By the autumn of 1918, with the situation on both the home and western fronts close to total collapse, and with her ships blockaded in home port by the British Grand Fleet, Germany could endure no more. Following the Kaiser's flight to neutral Holland in November 1918, the German government sued for peace, and when the armistice turned into unconditional surrender at Versailles the following June, it signified the end of Germany's maritime ambitions.

At the stroke of a pen virtually the entire German merchant marine became the property of the victorious Allies, and with loud calls by a very vocal majority that Germany should be made to pay "ton for ton" for every vessel that had been lost, the Government delegated the distribution of the British prizes to the Shipping Controller.

The huge 56,551 ton *Majestic* arrives at Southampton following her completion at Blohm & Voss shipyard at Hamburg. *Majestic* made her maiden voyage for White Star on 10th May 1922, nearly eight years after her launch. With her arrival, the company could once again claim to operate the largest steamer in the world.   *Paul Louden Brown Collection*

On 17th November 1919 the Admiralty sent the list of prize tonnage to the British shipping lines capable of operating such large ships and invited them to make tenders for their purchase. For Cunard, wholly under English ownership, there was no problem and in May 1920 they successfully completed the acquisition of the former HAPAG liner *Imperator* renaming her *Berengaria*. The Admiralty, however, were treating Cunard as something of a special case as the company had lost 22 vessels during the conflict, amounting to over 200,000 tons.

For the White Star Line, owned by the American IMM combine, the situation was less clear cut. The company's task of rebuilding White Star's pre-war passenger business was no less pressing than that of Cunard. The British Government, however, were understandably reluctant to allocate its war prizes to the company, as the IMM agreement to keep the ships of the formerly British companies on the British register and available for emergency service was soon to expire. At any time after 27th September 1922, IMM would be legally entitled to give five years notice to end the agreement and transfer their British ships to foreign registry. For the British Government the prospect of losing such hard won prizes to a foreign flag, no matter how friendly, could not be contemplated.

None of this helped to make Harold Sanderson's job any easier. A makeshift service between Liverpool and New York had reopened shortly after the end of hostilities, but the reinstatement of the Southampton to New York express service was much more difficult. The *Britannic*, *Oceanic* and *Titanic* were all gone, and the *Olympic* was conspicuous by her absence, being retained by the Admiralty to transport troops back to Canada. It was not until August 1919 that she was finally returned to Harland and Wolff for reconditioning as a

liner and conversion from coal to oil firing. Even then she would not return to commercial service until the following June.

The problem of a suitable running mate for the *Olympic* still remained and, with the projected two-to-three-year construction time combined with spiralling costs, the future for White Star did not look encouraging. At first there seemed to be little option other than to proceed with an expensive reconstruction programme as IMM were also reluctant to place any of their allocation of American prize tonnage on the British register. Then, on 2nd September 1919, an arrangement was reached in London whereby the White Star Line agreed to remain on the British registry for a further twenty years. Suddenly the speedy reconstruction of the fleet was possible.

Sanderson immediately began to scan the Admiralty list for suitable replacements for White Star's lost liners. By the time he had finished he had arranged for the purchase of three of the prize ships, starting with the former Norddeutscher Lloyd (NDL) liner *Berlin* which, renamed *Arabic*, joined White Star's New York / Mediterranean service in November 1920. Another NDL liner, the 34,356 ton *Colombus*, became *Olympic*'s first post war running mate on the Southampton to New York service, but it was the arrival of 56,551 former HAPAG liner *Bismarck*, suitably renamed *Majestic*, in the summer of 1922, that marked the full restoration of the Southampton service.

For the White Star Line the 1920s would mark a new beginning. The Great War was over and the *Titanic* debacle, although a painful memory, could finally be relegated to the pages of history. But, while the *Titanic* would never truly forgotten, memory of the *Britannic* faded. On 4th July 1919, the furniture, fittings and materials placed in storage at

Belfast in 1915 when the *Britannic* was requisitioned had been auctioned off and nothing remained of the ship itself.

The name, however, was not forgotten in the offices of the White Star Line and on 6th August 1929, the new 27,000 ton motor ship *Britannic* was launched at Belfast. The new ship, like the two previous vessels to bear the name, was one of the finest of her kind and so successful that a second ship of her class, the *Georgic*, was quickly ordered to join her in service on the White Star Liverpool to New York service.

History would dictate that the *Georgic* was to be the last White Star liner ever built and, although totally gutted by German bombs during the Second World War, she remained in service until being sold for scrap in 1956. The *Britannic* came through World War II unscathed, despite being temporarily abandoned by her escort, HMS *Rodney*, during the hunt for the *Bismarck* in 1941. She would go on to be the last White Star ship in the Cunard White Star fleet, formed when the two companies were merged in 1934. When the *Britannic* finally went to Inverkeithing for scrapping in December 1960, she marked the final passing of Thomas Ismay's ambitious plan of over ninety years earlier to make the White Star Line pre-eminent on the North Atlantic.

The end of the White Star Line, however, is not quite the end of the *Britannic*'s story.

Homeric (above) was *Olympic's* first permanent post-war running mate. At 34,351 tons and with a service speed of 18^{1}/$_{2}$ knots, she was never an ideal companion for the *Olympic* and *Majestic*, but she developed a reputation as one of the steadiest ships afloat.
Paul Louden Brown Collection

(*Left*) The name *Britannic* lived on until 1960 in the form of this vessel built in 1930 for the White Star Line.
From Liners in Art by Kenneth Vard, painting by Derrick Smoothy

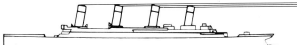

Chapter Nine
The Eighty Year Enigma

Despite her size and importance, wreck number 101502722 (the British Hydrographic Office's official wreck number for the *Britannic*) remained undisturbed in the Kea Channel for close on sixty years. In 1947 her position was officially recorded as being a little over 2.5 nautical miles west of Angalistros Point on the island of Makronisos, and in 1960 that position was more or less confirmed by the Admiralty to within a fraction of a degree. While, however, the official location of the wreck was clearly marked on the Admiralty charts, few considered exploration of the *Britannic* to be worthwhile. In spite of this apparent indifference, however, questions about the ship's sinking abounded.

The safety features incorporated into the *Britannic* as a direct result of the *Titanic* disaster ought, in theory at least, to have made the ship practically unsinkable. The inclusion of additional, stronger and higher bulkheads really did mean that the ship should have been able to float with her forward six compartments open to the sea, while the inner watertight skin, which ran for the full length of the engine and boiler room compartments, were ample evidence to just how much effort Harland and Wolff had made to correct the defects so clearly highlighted by the *Titanic*.

Yet in the end all this extra effort came to nothing. In 1912 the *Titanic* had taken over two and a half hours to die while her younger sister, supposedly even more unsinkable, had gone down in barely fifty five minutes. True, the scale of the damage from the explosion was far more serious than the 250ft long gash inflicted by the iceberg, yet the damage was also more localised and its effects should have been easier to contain. Other interesting questions arose: why, for example, irrespective of it being a mine or torpedo, was a single weapon enough to sink such a supposedly unsinkable ship? This riddle has provided conspiracy theorists with a variety of plots, ranging from illicit armaments in the cargo holds, to German sabotage, and even a clandestine British plot to deliberately sink the hospital ship. Although to some these theories may seem

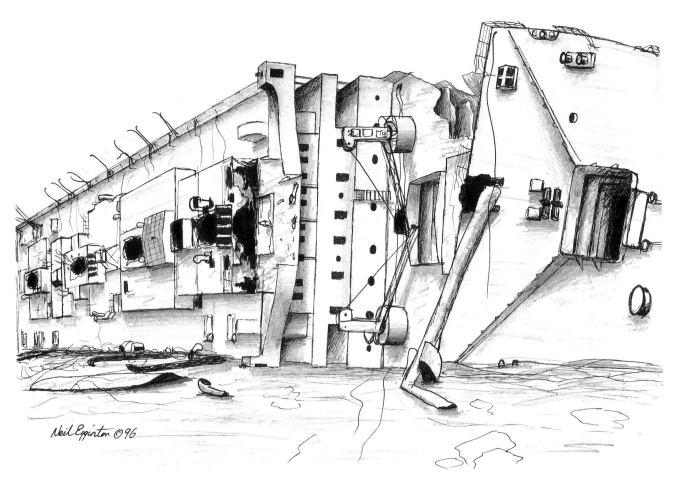

The bridge and other wooden structures are long gone yet, even after 80 years on the seabed, the coral encrusted hull of the *Britannic* is still remarkably intact.

Neil Eggington

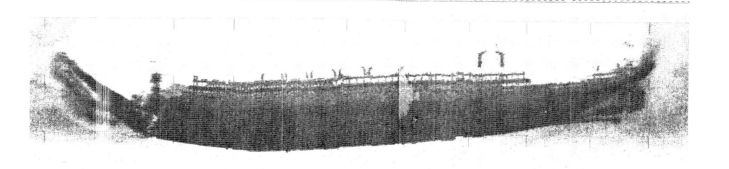

Sonar scan taken by the *NR-1* during the first days of the 1995 exploration of the wreck of the *Britannic*.

Robert Ballard/Hugh Brewster, Madison Press

just a little far fetched, a closer look at some of the details suggests that there could just be more to them than one may at first think.

The sabotage theory could be equally applied to both the Germans and the British. By 1916 the subversive activities of German agents had achieved a number of important successes, with a number of merchant and naval vessels exploding for no apparent reason, even in the supposedly impregnable Grand Fleet anchorage at Scapa Flow. Equally possible, though somewhat less probable, it could even have been the Admiralty who sabotaged the *Britannic*. At first glance this theory seems almost incredible, until we stop to consider that Britain stood to gain a great deal in the form of additional American sympathy for the Allied cause, not to mention the justification for a possible occupation of Greek territory on the pretence that the Greeks were incapable of ensuring the safety of foreign vessels in Greek territorial waters. It's tantalising to think of the possibilities but in the end neither sabotage theory is very likely. From our knowledge that the *U73* laid mines in the vicinity barely a month before the disaster, it is not difficult to come to the conclusion that the *Britannic*, like a great many other vessels of the era, was simply in the wrong place at the wrong time.

But why was the explosion so large? Smaller vessels had been known to survive similar blows from a single torpedo or mine. Once again the conspiracy theorists could home in on another dubious aspect of the disaster by implying that the scale of the damage was actually due to a massive secondary explosion caused by a hold packed full of illicit arms. Again it is possible, but all the surviving documentary evidence suggests that in 1916 the Admiralty were particularly keen to guarantee the safe passage of their hospital ships, taking specific steps to ensure that neither the personnel nor stores that they carried were for anything other than medical purposes.

The secondary explosion, however, is a pertinent issue, and we are left with the very valid question of what caused it if the *Britannic* was not carrying arms? The answer could well lie in the *Britannic*'s cargo manifest for the voyage, but as this is lost we can only speculate. That coal dust in the reserve coal bunker exploded is a well known and very

plausible theory, but it is possible that the *Britannic*'s cargo might indeed have been a major factor in her demise. The holds would certainly have been loaded with crates and medical supplies of every description, and part of that cargo could well have included large quantities of ether. All of us are aware of the medicinal qualities of this chemical, indeed it was a very commonly used anaesthetic at the time, but some people might be surprised to know just how volatile and highly flammable the substance can be. It is unlikely that the ether alone could account for the scale of the explosion, but it might have been present in large enough quantities to provide that all-important link in the chain that culminated in an explosion in the coal bunker.

For years these questions went unanswered until, in 1975, William Tantum of the *Titanic* Historical Society of America approached French oceanographer Jacques Cousteau about the possibility of diving on the lost ship. The idea appealed to Cousteau and, as he was already working in the Aegean on survey for the Greek Tourist Authority to locate the lost city of Atlantis, it was not long before his ship, the *Calypso*, was on station in the Kea Channel.

Cousteau finally located the wreck on 3rd December 1975, and immediately the *Britannic* presented her explorers with as many riddles as she had the historians. The satellite navigation position of 37° 42' 05" N, 24° 17' 02" E placed the wreck some 6.75 nautical miles (approximately eight statute miles) to the east of the position on the Admiralty charts and immediately questions arose as to why the position indicated on the chart was so far out. Perhaps the conspiracy theorists were right after all and the British Admiralty, who would be less than happy at the prospect of divers exploring the wreck and uncovering something which might prove embarrassing, had deliberately misplaced the wreck to make any attempts at finding it more difficult. If this is true then they nearly succeeded, because it took Dr. Harold Edgerton's sophisticated side-sweeping sonar to pinpoint the real location of the wreck, some three miles north west of Port St. Nikolo. Perhaps Cousteau should have placed more faith in Captain Bartlett's navigational skills, because the *Britannic* turned out to be more or less where he said she went down in 1916.

It was not until September 1976 that Cousteau was able to return to the Kea Channel to dive on the wreck and attempt to end the controversy once and for all. The logistics of the dive were formidable. *Britannic* was lying in 390 ft of water and the only way Cousteau and his divers could go so deep was by breathing a mixture of oxygen and helium. Even then, the extreme depth meant that each dive had to be limited to only fifteen minutes. The divers would then have to spend the better part of three hours in a decompression chamber before being allowed to return to normal atmospheric conditions.

With time at such a premium there was little time to waste once on the bottom, but although the divers made some 68 manned dives to the *Britannic*, bearing in mind the time it took to descend to the wreck and return to the submerged decompression chamber, they were left with barely five minutes per dive to explore the wreck. The total dive time on the *Britannic* herself probably amounted to something in the region of six hours, and the difficulty in obtaining any subsequent information from the Cousteau Society would seem to suggest that little of any lasting value was learned. A number of artefacts were retrieved, however, including part of the ship's wheel, the base of an engine telegraph and an officer's sextant.

Beyond that the *Britannic* was raising more questions than she had answered. Cousteau found no evidence to suggest that the *Britannic* had been carrying armaments of any kind, but the scale of the damage to the hull did explain why the ship had gone down so quickly. In the words of William Tantum, the hole was: "...so big that you could drive a car through it!" Cousteau's own sketches actually showed it to be far larger than even that, so huge in fact that much of the keel between the second and third bulkheads could not be located. The mass of twisted metal and the gaping hole beneath the forward well deck provided ample testimony as to just how extensive the damage really was and, once again, the exploding coal dust theory was revived. Reasoning that the point of impact was not only in the vicinity of the reserve coal bunker, but also that deposits of coal had been found some distance from the wreck, the evidence did seem to indicate that an initial blast could have instigated a chain reaction that virtually blew away the bows of the ship. The damage was so extensive that only a few remaining deck plates of B deck attached the fo'c'sle to the rest of the hull.

Cousteau's survey did turn up a number of points of interest, such as the nearby crushed flotation tanks belonging to one of the lifeboats smashed by the *Britannic*'s port propeller, however its limited scope meant that three of the funnels remained undetected. Of far more interest, however, was the missing section of hull plating. Where was it?

By the time *Calypso* finally left the Kea Channel Cousteau had provided a fascinating glimpse of the largest liner on the seabed, yet there were still a number of important questions to be answered. Even those points that had supposedly been addressed were as clouded by personal feelings as ever; Sheila Macbeth Mitchell, one of the nurses on the *Britannic*'s last voyage, was aboard the *Calypso* for part of the dive. Given the opportunity to view the coral-encrusted hospital ship from the *Calypso*'s small two-man submarine she joked with the pilot that she hoped there were no torpedoes on board this time. Some months later, when Cousteau gathered a number of survivors in London for a reunion dinner, few of them could bring themselves to accept that it was a mine that had been responsible for the disaster; the majority remained convinced that the ship had been deliberately torpedoed.

Twenty years on, the answer to whether a torpedo or mine sank the *Britannic* might finally be on the way. In the summer of 1995, Dr Robert Ballard, who ten years earlier had led the expedition which discovered the wreck of the *Titanic*, arrived in the Kea Channel to pick up where Cousteau had left off. While Cousteau's work had been limited by the available technology of the time, Ballard brought with him the latest state-of-the-art underwater remote operated vehicles (ROVs) and the *NR-1*, an American nuclear powered submarine. Ballard's pioneering work with ROVs had made the detailed mapping and examination of the *Titanic* wreck site possible, though the condition of the wreck itself had been a disappointment. The wreck of the *Titanic* is a mess: it lies in two major sections nearly 2,000 feet apart, joined by a large debris field consisting of the shattered central section of the ship and the internal fittings scattered as the hull disintegrated on its two and a half mile journey to the ocean bed.

The condition of the *Britannic*, however, was more encouraging. Twenty years after Cousteau's first visit the hull was still largely intact and, with the dynamic positioning capability of the base ship *Carolyn Chouest*, it was possible to position the ROVs over the wreck with pinpoint accuracy and keep them there for hours at a time. With underwater visibility of over 40ft the resulting images were stunning and showed the *Britannic* to be in far better condition than anyone could have hoped. Although most of the woodwork had long since rotted away, the wreck itself had hardly changed in the twenty years since Cousteau visited the site; the huge davits are still turned out as they had been when the ship sank; the glass over the first class staircase is still intact; the compass platform and nearly all of the deck railings are still in position and the three coral-encrusted propellers are intact. Several snagged fishing nets provided ample warning of the dangers of taking the ROVs in too close so it proved impossible to get a detailed look at the open watertight doors in the damaged area. The technology leap of twenty years, nonetheless, provided a view of the ship that, until recently, few would have thought possible.

Doctor Robert Ballard and the Expedition Coordinator Cathy Offinger. The memorial plaque they are holding now lies in the vicinity of the wreck site.

The SSV *Carolyn Chouest*, the base ship for Robert Ballard's 1995 expedition to the wreck of the *Britannic*.

The technology also brought the more personal side of the *Britannic*'s story into clearer focus. At various points on the wreck it was possible to see a number of coral-encrusted ropes suspended along the promenade decks and other sections of the ship. At first there seemed to be no obvious reason why these ropes should be there at all, until we recall Sheila Mitchell's observation when aboard the *Calypso*: she described how the *Britannic*'s matron had put up temporary rope barriers in an attempt to ensure that the men remained on one side, the nurses on the other, and that never the twain shall meet. After the *Britannic* had gone down some of Mrs Dowse's restrictive signs were seen floating in the water near Sheila's lifeboat, moving a more jocular occupant of the boat to comment: "I'm surprised the old dame didn't put a notice to say doctors and sisters shouldn't drown on the same side of the ship." Eighty years on those very ropes still hang exactly as they did when first erected, bearing silent testimony to the moral and social etiquette of 1916 – or those of the *Britannic*'s matron at least!

While the ROVs were getting in close, the *NR-1* was busy photographing the full length of the wreck and conducting the first thorough survey of the debris field. Only time spent in careful analysis of the thousands of photographs and hours of video tape in the follow-up to the exploration will reveal a more detailed picture of what might have happened, but already we have a clearer picture of how the *Britannic* died.

That the ship rolled over to starboard before sinking was already well known but, away from the wreck, Cousteau had been unable to locate more than one of the funnels. Tracing the debris field running to the north of

the wreck, it did not take long for the *NR-1* to locate and photograph the three missing funnels, enabling the historians in the expedition team to contemplate exactly how the ship disintegrated during her plunge to the seabed.

If the wreck of the *Britannic* has begun to give up some of her secrets, diplomacy and officialdom ensure that the full truth of her past might never be known. A number of documents in the Public Record Office at Kew containing references to the *Britannic* still remain closed, only serving to fuel speculation that the Admiralty could indeed have something to hide. Could it be that Messany's allegations of healthy troops being carried in the holds indicate that the Admiralty, if not exactly breaking the rules, was bending them slightly, and was the transportation of R.A.M.C. personnel on the fifth voyage in violation of the Geneva Convention?

Away from the grey area of who, or what, was permissible under the terms of the Geneva Convention, there are a number of other questions to be answered; such as, how could the position of the wreck be incorrectly plotted on two occasions, and, could there still be any trace of the mine anchor remaining? Analysis of the video tapes and photographic stills resulting from the Ballard expedition may help to provide some answers, though whether any future explorations will enjoy the benefits of an undisturbed wreck, as enjoyed by Cousteau and Ballard, is already open to doubt.

The anonymity of the *Britannic* was her greatest defence against salvagers until, in September 1995, the *Sunday Express* revealed details of a proposed salvage project being put together by a Greek consortium. Following the discovery of the *Titanic*, continuing expeditions to the wreck site have resulted in the ship being systematically stripped of many of

(*Above*) The 146ft American nuclear-powered submarine *NR-1*. Until recently, information of the *NR-1* was still classified, but since the end of the Cold War she has been used on several non-military scientific projects. In 1986 the *NR-1* was used to receeover wreckage from the space shuttle *Challenger*.

Voyager is lowered over the side of the *Carolyn Chouest* (*left*). This ROV was particularly useful because she incorporated a three-dimensional video camera system developed by NASA. With *Voyager*'s replacement cost of $250,000, the jungle of twisted wreckage around *Britannic*'s hull was a constant headache for the pilots.

her artefacts, and despite the outcry from many historians, the fact that the ship is non-military and lying in international waters means that there is very little that can be done to stop the desecration. The wreck of the *Lusitania* has been even less fortunate; salvagers actually blasted her huge bronze propellers free with explosive charges in an attempt to offset some of their costs.

Hopefully, the wreck of the *Britannic* will not suffer the same fate as those of the *Lusitania* and *Titanic*. Aside from her obvious connection with the *Titanic*, the salvage of the *Britannic*'s rusting hospital beds is hardly likely to offer the financial returns that would make such an expedition worthwhile. Nor does the *Britannic* enjoy the same aura of luxury and mystery attached to the *Titanic* and *Lusitania*, and this probably accounts for why the wreck has remained largely undisturbed for so long. The *Britannic* also lies well within Greek coastal waters and, having been a commissioned ship in the Royal Navy and a registered war grave, is protected by the British Government. To date the Greek authorities have also exercised strict diving controls over the wreck, and anyone bold or unwise enough to bring up artefacts without permission from a wreck protected by the 1986 Protection of

Military Remains Act could face a stiff legal battle. The most notable exception to date is the famous recovery of over £40,000,000. in gold from the wreck of the British cruiser HMS *Edinburgh* in 1981. In this case, however, the gold was the property of the Russian Government and the expedition took place before the 1986 Act was passed, but the salvagers still had to guarantee that the disturbance to the wreck itself would be minimal.

So what does the future hold for the *Britannic*? Technological developments have demonstrated all too clearly that today shipwrecks have no hiding place from properly equipped divers, and with the *Britannic* lying in such accessible waters she is more open to unauthorised violation than most wrecks. So is there any way to protect the ship?

Robert Ballard clearly thinks so. In his words the *Britannic* is: "the most preserved, most pristine ship I have ever seen", and if his vision of the ship's future ever comes to fruition then it could just ensure that she stays that way. Ballard's intention was not simply to survey the wreck and then leave, but to explore the possibility of placing remote cameras and lights on the hull to make the *Britannic* part of a projected underwater museum. The technology to turn this vision into a reality already exists, while the results could be transmitted to museums and also be made available to people in the comfort of their own home via the Internet. If the British and Greek authorities ever give their permission for such a venture, there is little doubt that protection by active preservation will provide a golden opportunity to ensure that the wreck of the *Britannic* will be spared the fate of the wrecks of the *Titanic* and *Lusitania*.

Hopefully, in the years to come, careful examination of the images from the 1995 expedition to the wreck will substantially add to our knowledge of the story of the *Britannic* and her all too brief life. Even though, after eighty years and two expeditions, the ship has yet to give up all her secrets, if the *Britannic* does eventually become a part of an interactive underwater museum then it is just possible that this forgotten sister of the Olympic class liners could become the most enduring.

The *Britannic* as she is today. With underwater visibility of around 40ft, it is not difficult to see just how large the *Britannic* is.
Neil Eggington

Appendix I

Britannic Building Details

Registered: At Liverpool as HMHS *Britannic* at noon on 8th December 1915. *Registered No:* 137490.
Net tonnage: 24,592 tons. *Gross tonnage:* 48.158 tons.
Displacement: 78,950 tons. *Length:* 852ft 6in (b.p.)
Beam: 94ft. *Moulded depth:* 64ft 3in. *Total height from keel to navigating bridge:* 104ft 6in. *Load draught:* 34ft 7in. *No. of decks:* 9. *No. of bulkheads:* 16.
Propelling machinery: 29 steel boilers, 215 psi. Two sets of inverted direct acting triple expansion engines. One low pressure turbine driving centre shaft.

No. and diameter of cylinders in each set of reciprocating engines: 1 @ 54in, 1 @ 84in, 2 @ 97in. *Length of Stoke:* 75in
IHP of reciprocating engines: 32,000.
SHP of turbine engine: 18,000.
Speed: 21 knots
Accommodation: 790 first class; 836 second class; 953 third class; 950 crew. Total complement: 3,529.
Registry closed: 18th December 1916, on advice from Henry Concanon.

Appendix II

Log of HMHS *Britannic*

Requisitioned as a Hospital Ship on 13th November 1915. Hospital Ship G618.

Leave:				*Arrive:*		
	Liverpool	23rd December 1915	12.20 am		Naples	28th December 1915
	Naples	29th December 1915	3.50 pm		Mudros	31st December 1915
	Mudros	3rd January 1916	3.35 pm		Southampton	9th January 1916
	Southampton	20th January 1916	11.51 am		Naples	25th January 1916
	Naples	4th February 1916	3.15 pm		Southampton	9th February 1916
	Southampton	20th March 1916	4.26 pm		Naples	25th March 1916
	Naples	27th March 1916	4.00 pm		Augusta	28th March 1916
	Augusta	30th March 1916	3.00 pm		Southampton	4th April 1916

12th April 1916: Laid up at half rate (5/- per gross ton).
21st May 1916: Discharged from service. White Star paid £76,000 to recondition ship. Arrived back at Belfast 18th May.
28th August 1916: Recalled for service as a hospital ship.

Leave:				*Arrive:*		
	Southampton	9th September 1916			Cowes	9th September 1916
	Cowes	24th September 1916	5.40 pm		Naples	29th September 1916
	Naples	1st October 1916			Mudros	3rd October 1916
	Mudros	5th October 1916			Southampton	11th October 1916
	Southampton	20th October 1916	4.30 pm		Naples	25th October 1916
	Naples	26th October 19196	4.42 pm		Mudros	28th October 1916
	Mudros	30th October 1916	12.05 pm		Southampton	6th November 1916
	Southampton	12th November 1916	2.23 pm		Naples	17th November 1916
	Naples	19th November 1916				

Sunk: 21st November 1916 in the Kea Channel on voyage to Mudros with loss of 21 crew and 9 men of RAMC (30).

Appendix III

Hydrographic Office Details of Wreck of SS *Britannic*

Wreck Number: 101502722
Position: Lat 37° 42' 05" N Long 24° 17' 02" E.
Quality of Fix: SATNAV (Satellite Navigation).
Horizontal Datum: European (1950) (ED50).
Name: Britannic. *Nationality:* British. *Type:* Steamship.
Tonnage: 48,158 gross. *Length:* 852ft 6in (b.p.). *Beam:* 94ft. *Draught:* 59ft. *Date sunk:* 21st November 1916.
Chart symbol: Non-dangerous wreck.
Charts (Navigational): 1630, 2682. *General Depth:* 110m.
Vertical Datum: Mean Low Water Springs.
Circumstances of loss: Vessel, built 1914 as a White Star liner, was taken over by Admiralty for use as hospital ship before completion. She was *en route* to Mudros with 625 crew and 500 medical officers to take on board wounded when she struck a mine in the Kea Channel laid by the German submarine *U73*. *Britannic* sank in less than one hour with the loss of 30 lives.
Surveying details: H2419/47. 15th May 1947. Non-

dangerous wreck in position 373900N 241000E. (C in C Med). 12th January 1960 European Position 373910N 240942E. H3592/73. 4th December 1975 wreck located and identified by *Calypso* (Commander Cousteau and divers) in satellite navigation position 374205N 241702E (EUR), lying in a general depth of 110 metres. Stated to have least depth of approximately 80 metres. (Telecom to W.O. 3rd December 1975 and U.W.I. letter 12739/4/4 dated 3rd December 1975).

Note from Hydrographic Office dated 13th September 1991 states that the Cousteau position is approximately 6.75 nautical miles northeast of the original position. No Notice to Mariners has been issued by the Greek Hydrographic Office who are the charting authority for the area. Because the wreck is not a hazard to surface navigation the change in position has only been included as a minor correction by the British Hydrographic Office and will appear on the next new edition of British Admiralty charts.

Appendix IV

Casualties of Sinking

Fatalities

Crew	Age	Rank	Home Town
R C Babey	24	Trimmer	Warsash, Hants
J Brown	40	Fireman	Manchester
T Crawford	27	4th Butcher	Tranmere
A Dennis	20	Trimmer	Southampton
F Earley	47	Leading Fireman	Southampton
C S Garland	35	Steward	Bristol
L George	17	Scullion	Southampton
P Gillespie	30	2nd Electrician	Liverpool
G Godwin	29	Fireman	Dorset
G Honeycutt	30	Lookout	Southampton
W Jenkins	39	2nd Baker	Egremont
J McFeat	29	Fireman	Southampton
C Phillips	24	Trimmer	Hampshire
G Philps	41	Fireman	Hampshire
J Rice	23	Steward	Liverpool
G Sherrin	45	Greaser	Southampton
W Smith	29	Fireman	London
T Taylor	24	Assistant Cook	Liverpool
A Toogood	48	Steward	Hampshire
T Tully	38	Steward	Roscommon
P White	19	Trimmer	Southampton

RAMC

Lieutenant J Cropper Sergeant W Sharpe
Private A W Binks Private G J Bostock
Private H Freebury Private T Jones
Private G King Private L Smith
Private W Stone

Total Killed: 30 – 21 Crew, 9 Officers and Men of RAMC

Wounded

At Russian Hospital, Piraeus

J Herring	Fireman
C Hughes	Steward
S Jenn	Mess Room Steward
J Kennedy	Scullion
W Kneller	Fireman
E Long	Engineer's Storekeeper
J McEvoy	Fireman
T Mitchell	Fireman
F Reed	Fireman
G Sherwatt	Laundry
C Sparkes	Fireman

In HMS _Duncan_ Sick Bay

R Bennett	Leading Fireman
H Carr	Steward
W E Green	Laundry
P Healey	Trimmer
H Keamish	Trimmer
J Smith	Steward
F Whitlock	Fireman

In Sick Bay of French Warship _Ernest Renan_

J Nolan Trimmer

In Sick Bay of French Warship _Patrie_

W Ridett Fireman

Stewardesses at Phaleron with Nurses

V C Jessop
C Kemp
E Murray
A M Skilling

Appendix V

The Career of Captain Bartlett

Born: 21st August 1868 (London)
Educated: Cowper Street School, London
Apprenticed: D Bruce Clippers, Dundee
Passed for Certificate: London, 1893
Ordinary Certificate No: 018359
Career milestones:
  1888:   Joined British India Company
  1894:   Joined White Star Line
  1907:   Royal Decoration. (R.N.R. retired)
  1912–14: White Star Marine Superintendent, Belfast
  1914:   Captain R.N.R. (22nd June)
  1914–15: Patrolling Duties in North Sea
  1916:   Elected Younger Brother of The Trinity
        House
  1919:   A.D.C. to H.M. the King (Until 1921)
  1920:   C.B.E. (Civil Division) for Services During
        the War
  1921:   Member of R.N.R. Advisory Committee
        Commodore on Retired List of R.N.R.
        (14th October)
  1931:   Mariner Warden of the Honourable
        Company of Master Mariners
Retired from White Star Line: 31st December, 1931
Died: 15th February 1945

Appointments(2nd Mate and above):

Ship	Reg No.	Appointed	Route	Rank
Jumna	93291	12.03.91	Med	2nd Mate
Dorunda	73759	26.04.93	East Indies	2nd Mate
Jelunga	98596	12.01.94	East Indies	2nd Mate
Doric	87847	15.06.94	Australia	2nd Mate
Gothic	102119	23.01.97	Australia	2nd Mate
Gothic	102119	17.03.98	Australia	1st Mate
Georgic	105326	29.03.00	U.S	2nd Mate
Georgic	105326	01.01.01	U.S	1st Mate
Teutonic	96334	20.02.01	U.S	1st Mate
Celtic	113476	04.10.01	U.S	1st Mate
Teutonic	96334	01.11.01	U.S	1st Mate
Oceanic	110596	18.03.02	U.S	1st Mate
Celtic	113476	11.05.03	U.S	1st Mate
Armenian	105338	29.10.03	U.S	Captain
Germanic	70932	22.04.04	U.S	Captain
Victorian	105334	06.12.04	U.S	Captain
Canopic	113408	19.04.05	U.S./Med	Captain
Gothic	102119	05.02.06	Australia	Captain
Republic	118043	25.07.06	U.S	Captain
Cymric	106989	04.09.06	U.S	Captain
Romanic	109441	02.02.07	U.S./Med	Captain
Cedric	115354	03.04.07	U.S	Captain
Britannic	137490	14.12.15	Hospital ship	Captain
Britannic	137490	04.09.16	Hospital ship	Captain

Bibliography

Anderson, Roy, *White Star*, Stephenson & Sons, 1964.

Ballard, Robert D. & Archbold, Rick, *Lost Liners*, Madison Press, 1997.

Beaumont, J. C. H., *The British Mercantile Marine During the War*, Gay & Hancock, 1919.

Beaumont, J. C. H., *Ships and People*, Geoffrey Bles, 1926.

Bonsall, Thomas E., *Titanic*, Gallery Books, 1987.

Eaton, John P. & Haas, Charles A., *Falling Star*, Patrick Stephens, 1990.

Fellowes-Wilson, V. S., *The Largest Ships of the World*, Crosby, Lockwood & Son, 1926.

Fleming, Revd John A., *The Last Voyage of His Majesty's Hospital Ship Britannic*, Marshall Brothers, 1917.

Gibson, R. H., *The German Submarine War: 1914-18*, Constable & Co Ltd, 1931

Griffiths, Denis, *Power of the Great Liners*, Patrick Stephens, 1990.

Haws, Duncan, *White Star Line* (Merchant Fleets in Profile 19), TCL Publications, 1990.

Hocking, Charles, *Dictionary of Disasters at Sea During the Age of Steam*, Lloyds Register of Shipping, 1969.

Janes Fighting Ships of World War I, Studio Editions, 1990.

Kludas, Arnold, *Great Passenger Ships of the World: Volume 1*, Patrick Stephens, 1975.

Maxtone-Graham, John (ed.) *Olympic and Titanic: Ocean Liners of the Past*, Patrick Stephens, 1970.

Moss, M. & Hume, J. R., *Shipbuilders to the World: 125 Years of Harland and Wolff 1861-1986*, The Black Staff Press, 1986.

Oldham, Wilton J., *The Ismay Line*, Journal of Commerce, Liverpool, 1961.

Plumridge, John H., *Hospital Ships and Ambulance Trains*, Seeley, Service & Co, 1975.

Rentell, Philip, *Historic White Star Liners*, Waterfront Publications, 1987.

Shaum, John H. & Flayhart, William H., *Majesty at Sea: The Four Stackers*, Patrick Stephens, 1981.

The Titanic Commutator, Titanic Historical Society, Quarterly Journal.

Williams, David L. & de Kerbrech, Richard P., *Damned by Destiny*, Teredo Books Ltd, 1982.

Acknowledgements

When this book was first published I was able to list a host of companies and organisations that had helped to make it possible. The Southampton and Merseyside Maritime Museum provided me with a marvellous starting point, while the British Library, National Newspaper Library, Science and Reference Library, Harland and Wolff, Guildhall Library and Public Record Office provided me with a wealth of information that only enforced un-employment in the ever-depressed British Film Industry could enable me to examine in such depth.

Since 1992 I have also been able to increase my ever expanding *Britannic* archive as a result of the generosity of friends and fellow enthusiasts around the world. From the UK, Paul Louden Brown continues to unearth photographs and illustrations from his immense collection which now grace all three of my books, Neil Eggington for his underwater sketches of the *Britannic* as she is today, Anthony Walsh was kind enough to send me a copy of Percy Tyler's manuscript, Mr. Harold Roberts kindly furnished me with additional information and the photograph of the late Captain Harry Dyke and Mr. Angus Macbeth Mitchell kindly allowed me to reproduce the photographs from the famous Sheila Macbeth Mitchell photograph album.

Still in Europe, from Germany Frank Gutmann has the uncanny knack of being able to turn up anything from the German archives whenever I happen to need it and I seriously believe that his enthusiasm for the *Britannic* outstrips even mine.

From across "the pond", my thanks to Edward Kamuda of the *Titanic* Historical Society (P.O. Box 51053, Indian Orchard, Massachusetts 01151-0053, USA) who is forever offering help and encouragement, Eric Sauder whose notorious "memos" ensure that I try to keep as close to the facts as possible, and particularly to Ken Marschall for whose help, support and efforts to include me on the 1995 expedition to the wreck of the *Britannic* I will always be grateful. Also my thanks to Hugh Brewster at Madison Press, Toronto, for allowing me to include the *NR-1* sonar scans of the wreck site.

Finally, my grateful thanks to Dr Robert Ballard and his logistics co-ordinator / wizard Cathy Offinger for finding room for me on the 1995 *Britannic* Expedition, and to the crew of the *Carolyn Chouest* and *NR-1* (too numerous to name) who helped to make it such an unforgettable experience. I never for a moment thought when this book was first published that it would enable me to go on such a momentous trip and I can only hope that, if Bob Ballard's plans of an interactive museum ever become a reality, you will be able to experience the same thrill that I did when I saw the *Britannic* for the first time.